Ingrid Trier

ABRA CADABRA

What I Say, Shall Be Done!

The „One-Phrase Method",
that Millions of People Transform Their Lives with

Bibliographic information from the German National Library:
The German National Library lists this publication in the German
National Bibliography; detailed bibliographic data is available on
the Internet at http://dnb.dnb.de.

© 2025 Ingrid Trier
Editing: LivingLanguage, Cologne/GER
Cover image: TORI@Shutterstock.com
Publisher: BoD · Books on Demand GmbH, Überseering 33,
22297 Hamburg, bod@bod.de, Germany
Print: Libri Plureos GmbH, Friedensallee 273, 22763 Hamburg,
Germany

ISBN: 978-3-7693-9964-6

For Kathi

Just Reformulate Your Life!

The Three Laws of Transformation

The 1st Law

Abracadabra in practice

Smoke-Free & Slim

Calm down

Magically Slim Yourself Down

In Conclusion:

"In the Beginning Was the Word...;
...and the Word became Flesh."
John 1:1-4

~~~

In Hebrew, *abre ke dabra* Means:
"I Will Create as I Speak."

Abrakadabra

Life Does What the Spirit Tells It

Germany in May 1945,
the end of World War II in Europe.

My father was nine years old and one of the many children who were separated from their families as part of an "extended children's evacuation" from the war zone of the big cities to the countryside and thus to safe areas. There, in a foreign country, he and his two younger siblings waited for the opportunity to return home and be picked up by their mother. His father would not come to him because he had already died at the front.

Soon peace seemed to be at hand, and the children who had been sent away were finally allowed to go back to their parents. But they did not know that a lot had changed in their cities in the meantime and that the war was continuing at home in other ways.

My father was not picked up. His mother, who had meanwhile become engaged to another man, lost interest in her children and left them behind in the countryside. She was expecting the birth of a new baby, and this required all her attention. However, my father and his siblings were later forcibly returned to her, and she was asked to fulfill her duties and receive the children. The baby was born, but the relationship with the new man did not last long and my grandmother was now left alone with four children. Without any professional training, she had to earn her living and that of her children as a cleaner and later as an assistant in a nursing home. The family was poor and further traumatized by the war. My father's motto in life was fitting:

Living means suffering!

As the eldest son, he felt obliged to provide for the family and as he grew older, he began to look for jobs to earn money for food and the most basic things. He therefore had to forget a childhood of his own.

These experiences influenced his further life, which was often marked by sadness and pessimism, to such an extent that poverty and depression continued in an ongoing loop like a self-fulfilling prophecy and showed no improvement.

What he believed in and what he expressed, what he said, in conjunction with an environment that reflected this, produced the corresponding results.

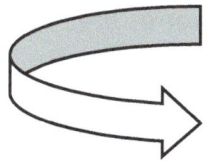 belief system +
habits + environment
→ material result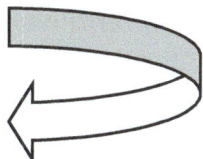

The "vicious circle" is formed. Due to the habit that causes ingrained thinking and behavior, we usually remain trapped in this bad cycle until we recognize this and bring about concrete changes.

His human disappointments led him to further beliefs, which he consistently passed on to his children. And because he kept repeating these sentences to himself and others, he could not progress in his life, could not achieve more than what these sentences, like a route description for the rest of his life, gave him. Detached from structure and role models, exposed to a life without opportunities, he lost all perspective in his youth. Later he met my mother, who came from a good background, and she chose him, despite warnings from her parents, who wanted better for her than a boy from the lower class. Since he now had a new environment with more positive examples, his sentences also improved over time:

With hard work and discipline, you get further in life.

He slowly got his life under control; he started an apprenticeship and worked his way up in the company. But the demons from back then did not let go of him and so he continued to lack a feeling of security. With the responsibility for four children of his own, he always knew that he would not be able to make ends meet financially. So, he tried gambling. Being able to be a child, playing and forgetting everyday life and at the same time dreaming of big money - the big run on the slot machine. Sometimes he managed it, but mostly he lost what little he had.

The answer to his children's question about the fulfillment of their wishes was always a consistent no. Membership in a sports club, taking part in an outing with friends, buying a pet or simply new clothes - the answer was already known in advance: No. Such crazy things as the desire to attend high school or even study at a university one day were always answered with the same sentence:

That's only for the rich, we can't afford it!

Another fatal sentence, a family mantra that steers life in directions in which chronic financial bottlenecks mutate into a permanent "fate". Changes only occur when you change the sentence. And when you do, it seems like magic. But it is just a reformulation of a few words that then redirect the course for the rest of your life.

I had learned early on that having to worry about money every day was part of life, just like my father. It was his fears and anxieties that he passed on to me; I hadn't inherited much more from him. Both my parents have worked for as long as I can remember. Despite having four children, my mother always had to work too. With working parents, there would have been enough money. Unfortunately, my father had developed a gambling addiction that always led him to the pub after work and at weekends in the hope of winning big. The 1970s were the age of slot machines and people from humble backgrounds saw no prospect of making a career and earning a good income. Lottery and slot-machines gave them hope for a richer living. It was mainly the media of the 1970s that helped people become addicted to gambling with catchy, constantly repeated slogans. But because they always said to themselves:

You'll win big <u>someday!</u>

– their dreams never came true, because life is always now and knows no "someday".

Inheritance of Parental Dependence

One Saturday my father was supposed to buy groceries for himself and the family. At that time the shops closed at around 2 p.m. He came back in the afternoon and didn't have any shopping bags with him. My mother asked where the food was and where he had been. He said he had been in the pub. And he hadn't done any shopping. The money? In the slot machine. Everything gone. And there was no way of getting any more money from anywhere and the shops were closed until Monday.

My mother had to ask her parents for groceries again, as she did before. This behavior was also passed down through the generations, because my mother's parents had to leave their bombed-out apartment in Cologne/Germany during the war and seek refuge in their parents' house.

Inheritance of (a Lack of) Coping Strategies

At some point it couldn't go on like this anymore, my parents divorced - and they did this with great fanfare. The separation happened in the same way that my father had experienced with his own parents. His mother had turned away from her former husband and told him of her intention to divorce during the war while he was on leave from the front. He then went back to the war front with the desperate intention of not returning from the war alive. Here we had our own domestic war, which caused a lot of suffering.

After separating from my mother, my father also didn't want to live any longer. His attempts to end his life failed, however, and left to deal with the problem on his own, he had to reorganize his life, whether he liked it or not.

*"You never have any help,
you must deal with everything on your own."*

Self-fulfilling prophecies are passed down across generations if you pass on the wrong words. Wrong sentences that you keep repeating to yourself lead to misleading emotions, which then trigger appropriate but unfortunately unfavorable actions that harm you. And it was just a simple sentence, but it can sometimes lead to a whole series of harmful chains of events. They are false ideas that are stored in memory paths through the mechanism of repetition in a learning process.

"Life is hard. You always must fight!"

And how can life be anything other than hard? When you start to question the credibility of the sentences you have memorized and compare them with reality, you realize that these sentences often have nothing to do with the here and now. If you look around in this world, you realize that there is basically no shortage, but quite the opposite, abundance, excess and wealth. There is more than enough of everything. The resources are there, but how societies, governments, groups and communities distribute them is sometimes a matter of a different story. So, you have the choice of believing in the lack or in the amount of money, food and everything that is necessary to sustain life that actually exists in the world. And then the sentence can be:

"Great abundance!
There is enough of everything, more than enough, and
more and more of it is coming my way!"

If you repeat this over a certain period of time, the brain learns to store this content so that it does not have to remember it again and again. The first changes become noticeable, at school, at work or in your private life, when new imprints take their influence within the framework of the brain-body-environment axis. However, if you believe too soon that everything is in the bag and you can stop repeating sentences, the old fears may return over time, as if they had been lurking somewhere, so that they can once again take control of your thoughts and feelings.

If you allow yourself to do this for a short time and give them a little space, you will soon see the negative results on the outside again. Decisions become more hesitant, financial insecurities return, life seems to become more difficult again. Income decreases, opportunities do not arise, orders are canceled, a new, unpleasant chain reaction begins. Old memory paths do not disappear so easily. They are too deeply rooted for that.
New routines must be established, but everything begins quite simply with just one word. And then you start again:

"I am so happy about the abundance in my life. There is more of everything, more than enough and it is getting more and more and more every day!"

Let's replace the old words with new words and believe them so that our lives can take an enriching turn.

And when things then change, it feels like magic. But basically, it is pure science. Nothing is easier than thinking up, formulating, storing and learning simple words. If you choose your words and sentences well, they bring abundance, friendship, love, wealth and trust - everything that the outside world should provide. It does, but now we are not addressing our requests to it, but to ourselves. An invisible body-brain-environment connection ensures via internal channels that the words we say to ourselves and that flow into our memory through constant repetition - and from there work like magic in our lives.

"What I say, shall be done!"

Then experience how many miracles life has in store for you. How many miracles could happen for children who turn their sad sentences into good ones, who try to turn the bad into good after war and personal suffering, instead of believing the fallacy of thinking that the more you think about the misfortune, the faster you can process it, or that the memory of bad days and times is a fate that weighs on your shoulders forever? This is not the case; it does not have to be that way.

The Inheritance of Thinking Mainly Negatively

The memory is just a thought, the past has no reality and what comes in the future is largely decided and controlled by yourself if you set the course for a better and healthier life in the now with a biochemically well-balanced inner state. The hormone balance has an immense influence on the body and psyche, so that we can take a steering role here with conscious, healthy and self-promoting thinking.

What could be easier than putting together a few mantras, reading them every morning, for example, and letting them inspire you throughout the day? Or you spend a fortune on therapy, only to be confronted again and again with old tragic stories and feelings that trigger negative biochemical effects in the body, so that you never get out of the vicious circle of bad feelings and thoughts.

If I spend the next 10-15 minutes thinking about sad events, be it from my own life, or thinking about the death of whales and dolphins, the wars in the world, starving children in Africa, neglected children all over the world, and so on, then I encourage the release of stress hormones that flood my thoughts and feelings and drag me down mentally in a whirlpool of sadness and anger. The feeling that I physically feel is not pleasant. The body suffers when we indulge in bad thoughts. The body reacts with stress through sweating, heat, trembling, nausea, headaches and stomach aches and so on. We trigger all of this when we brood. But that also means that we have a lot of control over ourselves and our vital functions. We can use this knowledge and make it our own. Especially since with good as well as bad vibrations within us we attract the appropriate vibrations from outside to us in a completely natural way.

So when we think good things, motivate ourselves, are happy or even just grateful and content, then completely different hormones are released than when we do the opposite: think bad things, can't pull ourselves together, think about negative things from the past and live the day unhappily, thereby sending a biochemical message outwards that immediately comes back to us as an unpleasant echo. It influences the mood of others if you approach them in a grumpy manner and it also has effects on life itself, because here the unhappiness that you send out comes back to the sender as a chemical reaction via biochemical channels and connections to the outside.

The American singer Bobby McFerrin postulated this in his global hit:

"Don't worry, be happy!"

„**...when you worry, your face will frown, and that will bring everybody down, so don`t worry, be happy. "**

That's why it's not even bad advice to try to convince yourself to be happy, if necessary, even if you don't feel that way now. Being unhappy can become a bad habit and it will probably be difficult to break this state. Negativity can also be attractive and attracts pessimistic people and doomsayers in particular. The motto here is to resist.

There are many ways to cheer yourself up. Brooding, doubting, being afraid, trying to predict the worst has never helped anyone. Bad sentences that express dissatisfaction only make everything worse and intensify the bad mood. Stress hormones are released and ensure that you have unhappy feelings as well as unhappy thoughts. Good sentences increase the release of positive hormones that trigger good feelings and can give people a mood of peace and self-love.

Why don't we always choose the good feelings when they can already be created through words and sentences. Biochemical processes in the body determine how you think, how you feel, what kind of life you lead and how successful you are. Using these natural resources of the body and building a new present on them begins with a clear intention to do so. A construct of plans about how you want to redesign and change your life, a series of sentences that fit in with this and become deeply ingrained in your thoughts through daily repetition, all of this can change the biochemistry in the body for the better. What was pure mysticism for people in earlier years, decades and centuries is now increasingly coming out of the corner of "secrets", is more scientifically explainable than ever before and can be moved into the realm of the explanation through epigenetics, the formulas of electromagnetism and constructivist philosophies.

Why should we talk about secrets when we already know the truth?

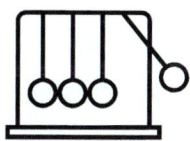

Constructivism

From Word to Sentence, from Sentence to Matter

The world is as you look at it. So many people, so many points of view.

In the beginning there was the word, and everything else arose from that - it became "flesh", or one could say *matter*. Nothing exists without a word that came before it, a plan that was formulated, a verbalized thought that was put into action. So, if change is to happen, where else could and should you start than with your own words? Where plans fail, where goals are not achieved and one often doesn't even start to set out on the path, the error usually lies in the learned (belief) statement.

What you say to yourself, what you say to the outside world and to others, ultimately determines how you live and how or who you are. Transformation always happens when you change your mantra, for better or for worse. Much more importantly, when the ideas of myself and the world out there, stored deep in my mind through constant learning processes, physiologically speaking as engrams or memory paths, are lived out anew every day, you often hardly notice, out of sheer routine, that you are only harming yourself.

How to Communicate Effectively with People

Routine words and sentences that you constantly say to yourself almost unconsciously, and then act accordingly, can turn into great profit or great failure. Words are like pure magic; they can change everything we want to change. That can be good, but also bad, depending on how you choose the sentences, how you are made and which, sometimes unconscious, guidelines you follow. You read that right - words can save relationships, but they can also destroy them. They have a great influence, both on how we interact with each other and on the life we lead.

If I say to someone: "Good morning!", there is a high probability that the greeting will be returned to me in the same or similar form. Even an appropriate apology at the right moment in a deadlocked relationship is often the turning point in situations where you think it's all over. Compliments initiate relationships, continue them and refresh contacts that had already died down. Insults, on the other hand, can be like a stab in the heart and cause the same relationships to end unexpectedly in the shortest possible time.

A friend of mine didn't feel comfortable in her marriage for a while. She told me that when her husband came home from work, he would come into the house, say hello to her, take off his shoes in the hallway and then disappear into the study with his briefcase because he still had work to do. Later he would come into the living room, and they would have dinner together. After that he would disappear into the study again. This was usually the case every day. She wished that when he came home, he would sit down with her for a moment and talk to her about the day, instead of always running away.

I told her that if she wanted to change something, she had to change herself first. She wanted a loving relationship, then she had to become loving. Because she herself always sat in the same place at the table in the afternoon and waited for her husband to come home and cheer up her life, she didn't have much more than a quick hello in return when he entered the house and greeted her from 4 meters away. I told her that what she wanted, she had to give first - she had to turn into the woman who gives attention before demanding it. Then, the next time he came home from work and stood in the hallway for a moment and took off his shoes, she went up to him and told him how nice it was to see him and that she had made him his favorite after-work drink. And you can imagine that he then sat down at the table with her for a while and talked to her about the day's events. And so, they continued every day. But it's not just about how you talk to others - it's primarily about how you talk to yourself.

How to Communicate Effectively with Life

In fact, once you have internalized the right sentences, you no longer need external attention, you become free and independent and what you are striving for comes by itself. The desire for more attention is understandable, but ultimately it only shows that you have not given yourself enough of it, so you project the desire outwards. The less you care about yourself, the more someone else should do it. But as other grown people are only responsible for their personal needs, you will have to care about your own needs as well. On the other hand, new problems would arise and people would stay away from you because they don't want to take responsibility for another adult.

Why was she sitting alone at this table waiting for him to come home from work? Basically, she should have just done something nice or interesting with her time in the afternoon, something that reflected her loving approach to herself. Then he would have been surprised not to see her sitting at the table anymore and might have come up with the idea of checking on her himself. Because of the expectations that she exuded every day in the same situation at home after work, he knew that he couldn't do anything right and so, perhaps unconsciously, he always retreated straight to his study.

So there are the words that you address to the outside world, but much more exciting are the words that you address to yourself and thus change your life without having to do much, because secret inner paths that connect us with our environment channel what we think of ourselves out into the world and appear as a hunch, as a feeling in the other person. Our feelings are noticeable to the world and to the people in it. We make ourselves known in many ways, others notice through smells when we are afraid or excited, happy hormones influence the other person and the world in which we live. The other person can react to us and the world itself can react to us. The latter is the more mysterious.

How does it happen, how does it work? We are usually not aware of how much power is contained in our words. We don't think about it and just talk and feel as we please. Words and feelings have clear effects, they have a certain effect on us and on our environment. This results in consequences that we can control if we choose our words and feelings more carefully.

Communication with the Environment and Its Effects

If words that I say to others have the effect that they come back to me in the same or similar way, then I am trying to be friendly to people so that they are usually friendly to me too.

- If I speak to others, they react to me.
- If I speak to myself, life reacts to me.

If I expect more from my life, I should not direct my expectations outwards, but on the contrary, inwards. The inner world of a person interacts with the outside world, sending signals in the form of verbal or non-verbal communication to others on the one hand

and through conversations, words, sentences, directed at oneself - on the other hand, communication with life itself, because a person's life takes place first and foremost in his or her brain, thinking and perception.

Psychological representatives of the scientific theory of *Radical Constructivism* postulated a stringent subjectivity in relation to the perception of reality and/or "real" reality. We would all live exclusively in a world of our own construction, based on experience. However, it has now become clear that if that were the case, we would not be able to exchange ideas with others about shared realities from our separate world and our brain, which was thought to be the center of our world. This could not exist alone without the body, possibly connected to machines, and experience perception. The brain needs the connection to the body in order to function. External impressions that I perceive are first sent to the brain via my sensory organs and from there filtered into the individual areas of thought.

Every person has a connection, a social interaction with the outside world. And this world is usually family, friends, colleagues, the job, the smaller and larger microcosm in which we live. We establish contact with others through our language and/or through looks, gestures and facial expressions. Habits arise from the fact that we always meet the same people, take the same route to work and buy our food in the same supermarket.

Communication with Yourself and Its Effects

But what about the words I say to myself? What response do I get, who answers me and how can I perceive it? If I keep telling myself in uncertain times that everything is fine and then it happens just like that, who set this in motion? Who is responsible, who heard my self-prayer?

If I say something to myself and repeat it like an over and over mantra that includes my needs and goals, I thereby establish a social interaction with life itself via a *brain-body-environment connection*, because I am my life, I live in my world (without the radical approach, that one *could not perceive anything outside of it*) and in self-communication I naturally have both a direct connection to myself and my world and an indirect connection to myself and my world. Thoughts flow consciously and unconsciously. Both processes have their own effects and should therefore be nurtured.

We Construct Our Lives Largely on Our Own

Unconscious thoughts have been pushed into non-conscious areas of thought by old beliefs. From there, they can lead a powerful life of their own. You can recognize this in behaviors that you want to stop but can't. Statements that are made without thinking and routines that you find good or bad, but you must make an effort to stop them or, if necessary, to redirect them into effectiveness.

If the outside world is analogous to the inside world, i.e., opposite it, then my world can do nothing other than reflect to me what I have repeatedly planted in my life field through words and actions. You shape the future from what you have experienced. We think that if we have burned our hand on the hot stove, we shouldn't touch it again - so far so good. But we also think that when the stove is cold - so far, so bad, because now we are creating a disturbed world of our own that must struggle with unrealistic fears and anxieties, even if everything is still open in the future and we cannot know what will happen. We all do that, and we all live that way because it is a precautionary measure of the brain; it wants to protect us so that we do not have to go through certain experiences again. And unfortunately, it happens exactly as we feared, because fear is a highly emotional process that channels what we fear into our lives via our inner *brain-body-environment connection*. Communication, thoughts mixed with strong feelings, is direct contact with the "lock". (More on this in the chapter: "A secret connection: body, mind and environment").

Here we are dealing with the insight that the life we lead, the life we perceive, as well as all other external impressions and influences, represents a pre-filtered compilation, a mosaic of things, people, places, which we seek out, visit, repeat again and again for various emotional reasons, whether it is to enjoy the contact or to work through possible traumas. We often use our words without thinking, and only when the damage is done do we take them back or accept that they have influenced our lives as a subtle weapon, sometimes to our advantage, sometimes to our disadvantage. Words have power; they change life situations.

And the same is true of the words we say to ourselves, not knowing that these are often phrases and expressions we have copied from our parents. Prejudices, opinions about others, learned rules, dislikes, worries – our own views are often just a repetition of what the microcosm of parents, other family members, but also teachers and educators or neighbors had passed on to us:

*"On Saturdays you must wash your car
and on Sundays you must visit your family."*

*"It's better not to stand out in this world – neither positively
nor negatively!"*

All of these are affirmations that guide people in a certain direction. It's no wonder that this can lead to great dissatisfaction, because you don't live what you yourself think of the world but rather continue to live the attitude of other people and of course their individual worldview. This may be right and consistent for them, but that doesn't apply to everyone else, and not to their children either, because they have a right to their own lives with their own worldview.

When you talk to yourself, you talk to the world – your world. And who answers you then? Of course, your world. If someone is looking for a new job and searches through job boards, sends applications, has interviews and then signs a work contract, for him or her this is communication with the world outside. If, on the other hand, someone relies on the fact that it is enough to tell themselves every day that they are professionally successful, have their dream job and no longer must search, the brain does not recognize the difference between reality and fiction.

A Different Perspective Reveals New Realities

It opens the "lock" of the *brain-body-environment connection* to the outside world and offers opportunities, as if the person had actively attracted the opportunities through their actions. You are no longer communicating with companies, but with life itself; it is a new way of contacting yourself, your subconscious and its power to make what was previously invisible visible. Because everything is there in this world. The filtering function of our sensory organs means that we concentrate on what fits our thoughts and our inner attitude and do not look where we do not find what is in harmony with us.

We do perceive these impressions but then classify them as inappropriate and push them out of our wider field of vision. However, as soon as we do, often after changing the way we evaluate life, we see a new world. If it weren't for these old, familiar sentences that we have always said to ourselves, perhaps because we learned them from our parents. Then you follow your routines, see corresponding things on the outside that fit exactly with them, but you don't really feel comfortable with them.

You feel good with the sentences that are your own. You can recognize these by the fact that they feel good and right and make you happy. If you notice an attitude in your thinking that feels bad, it is often an adopted mantra, an attitude "inherited" from others, which in many cases is anything but good. And what the person says brings the appropriate reflection into their life. So, if you say something bad, the people around you are not particularly happy about it. If you say something good, the recipients are happy about the positiveness that is shown to them.

Forward-Looking Self-Talk

And then there are the words you say to yourself. They also reflect everything and everyone you face outside. What you say to yourself comes back to you as a kind of echo of your environment. It is not only the words you say to others that can reflect, but also the words you say to yourself. Here, however, no person answers you, because the words are not addressed to a person outside of yourself - here life itself answers. Why have people for centuries and millennia said prayers that are reminiscent of a self-talk, addressing a higher power outside of themselves? Whatever you call this power, everyone can decide for themselves. Perhaps the definition or clarity of who or what answers is not all that important. Because basically it is about being able to establish this inner connection in the first place and thereby work out a plan for your individual life path and communicate it to the appropriate place with the necessary power.

Your words, especially if they are emotionally formulated, find a counterpart in your immediate environment and come back to you like a *boomerang*, hitting you either positively or negatively, depending on how you treat yourself, what you think of yourself, how you talk to yourself inside. If your relationship with yourself is rather clouded, others see it that way too. If you have a positive attitude towards yourself, you will receive an external reflection that matches it and reflects it accordingly.

This is the key if you want to change, control and improve things that happen to you. All you need is simple exercises, which I will show below. Words create feelings: "I am good the way I am!" said repeatedly, over days, weeks, until it becomes a memory path, leads to the right feeling, leads to the right echo from outside, leads to a life that is shaped by your own ideas and not by the dictates of others. The outside world doesn't care at all how we see ourselves, it only reflects the messages we send out from within. All the unfriendly or friendly people out there, the successes and failures, the generous and the exploiters are ultimately a reflection of our own feelings, which hold up a mirror to us in the form of people, things and situations.

Putting Aside Foreign Thought Patterns

That doesn't mean that if you are always generous, you automatically meet people who are just like you. Unless it is done out of selflessness. And if someone does take advantage of you, you will notice and protect yourself. But often you give something to others and secretly hope that you will get a little love and attention in return. Or that you will make a good impression or win over people who are not actually interested in contact.

So, what exactly is it about the fact that we can use our thoughts, our subconscious, our feelings to shape life the way we always wanted it to? The human brain apparently has "magical" powers. It is connected to the outside world via waves and invisible connections and focuses mainly on what it considers important and interesting based on its imprint. However, since every brain has specific limitations learned through upbringing and the environment, we only ever achieve in life what our brain considers possible and plausible.

We cannot and do not want to use anything else or only perceive it to a limited extent - we are limited in the absorption of things that we literally have no connection with. If we fail in certain areas, the cause is often a mixture of how we think and act and the decisions we make accordingly. And the way we think is the result of external influences, words and sentences that we have heard too often, so that they have seeped into our subconscious (learning processes) and now control our lives from that place. That can be good or bad. If we have often heard:

"You are great, you will go far!"

…we will most likely not live in slums and must fight for every crumb. At times we have been moved in advantageous directions, so that the high opinion and expectations of our first caregivers come true and we really achieve something. In this case, good sentences are usually spoken by people who have a positive self-image and like to encourage their children to see themselves positively too. If, on the other hand, we have learned:

"You are good for nothing,
you will never amount to anything!"

...the brain reacts here too and learns the content completely neutrally through repetition, because such sentences are constantly repeated by the people in question (who have then unconsciously expressed their opinion about themselves) because they again unconsciously hope that they will transfer their own feelings of uselessness to someone else and thus get rid of it forever.

The Downward Spiral of False Beliefs

But because this does not work so easily, they must convey the negative words again and again. This creates a bad spiral of humiliation and devaluation. At the expense of the child, such caregivers (parents, grandparents, teachers etc.) manage to create a feeling of relief for the moment, but this does not last long, so that the damaging affirmations must be repeated promptly and sadly this type of satisfaction can be felt again and again.

When the child, who is initially at the mercy of dependency and helplessness, now shows the first signs of feelings of inferiority, the speaker gets confirmation that he or she is better than the person close to him or her, who now must bear the burden of the "inherited" feeling of inferiority on their shoulders. But the care-givers are not free from this; they must continue to accept poor self-image until they begin to reflect on it and work on it in a con-crete way. The child is initially shaped and, because of the nega-tivity and self-doubt that cling to it, hopefully quickly, over the course of life, it will come to the point where it realizes that it must work on itself so that life can become better, healthier and more pleasant. But first, as the child grows up and in adulthood, it makes decisions and actions based on the fatal inspirations and influences of the parents' home and environment.

It is time, if you have not already done so, to say goodbye to this unpleasant legacy. As soon as you have understood the effect behind all the words and sentences from back then, you can iden-tify, understand and classify the failures, the misfortunes, the complications in your own life and avoid them in the future by formulating new sentences that bring about better things in life. A good and happy life awaits you if you use the miracle of your brain, establish new, special words and sentences that feel and work like magic spells, but work on a scientifically explainable level.

For the magic to work, a few small conditions must be met:

- absolute trust in the words and phrases chosen
- the formulation in the here and now, the language of the brain
- the use of positive adjectives that generate emotions
- speaking in the superlative, because you strive for the best and not the better:

"I am so happy that I am

- wealthy and healthy
- getting and keeping the new great job
- paying off my debts and never getting any more
- open to a new relationship
- able to sleep well every night

We must not doubt, then we will only experience uncertainty again, because if you don't believe in something, the brain will also be able to motivate the subconscious to make things happen according to our ideas. Three elements are therefore indispensable in any case to make the "magic" happen. How else could you produce a positive feeling that necessarily acts as an invisible glue between the conscious and subconscious mind, allowing the message to sink into the depths of the brain? If you say: "I want to be rich one day!", the brain keeps pushing the message back to "one day".

"*Today* I am absolutely happy that I managed to...!"

In this way, you can change important areas of your life, redesign them and shape them the way you always wanted, regardless of what others had planned for you.

The old thought patterns are difficult or sometimes never to be eliminated forever. But you can add new patterns that, through constant repetition, become more powerful over time than the old, useless imprints. The weakened imprints that were harmful and did not help you can, however, keep reappearing if we are triggered accordingly, we lose faith in a better life, give up on ourselves and neglect working on our own personality. They are in the back of our minds and can always come back onto the stage of life when we become weak and allow old demons to take over. Your life belongs to you, take it into your own hands. Even if others were entrusted with your upbringing at the beginning and automatically gave you their stamp of right and wrong, you now decide how things will continue for you. And everything you need for this is already inside you.

Use your natural resources and start living the way you always wanted to. The first step is to change the sentences that are already working within you, which you can reformulate exactly as you want. Choose them as you would on the day you achieved your goals.

Then you wake up and say to yourself:

"It's already done and I'm absolutely happy about it!"

Summary of the basic thesis:

We communicate with people on the one hand and with life itself on the other. Both have their respective effects:

In variant 1, the effect is shown as a response in the communication and/or actions of your counterpart.

In variant 2, the effect is also shown as a response in the communication and/or actions of your counterpart, who is now not a person, but life itself.
I can talk to the people around me. In communication, I talk to you, and you answer me/react to me.

I can also talk to myself. That is also communication. But now life answers me, it reacts to me through results, people, things, situations, experiences, apparent coincidences.

That sounds like magic, but it is quite easy to see through. Because - we humans have our self, which turns outwards and interacts with others - people, things and the environment. In addition, our self has different forms:

• the *social self* interacts with people in the environment

• the *ecological self* interacts with things in the environment and with nature

• the *basic self* is the interaction between the brain, body and the environment (what the body experiences through objects creates moods and affects in the brain)

In Resonance with People and the Whole World

The brain does not produce the mind, the mind shapes the brain. The brain is therefore a matrix of experiences. This can be seen in newborns, who imitate the facial expressions of their caregivers - the US developmental researchers Andrew Meltzoff and M. Keith Moore defined this as "expression imitation" back in the 1970s. There you will find an interplay of physical expression, gestures and emotional resonance. These external impulses can be seen as overarching effects of an interpersonal "space" that the people experience together. If everyone only lived in their own world, this would not be possible - we view reality subjectively, but for that to happen, it must first exist, i.e. objectively.

The German psychotherapist Thomas Fuchs describes this phenomenon as "interbody resonance". This term is intended to describe the fact that our bodies are always in exchange with one another as soon as we are sufficiently close to one another, even if this often escapes our attention. If we are connected to the body and the environment via the brain, emotion could appear as an overarching phenomenon on a non-physical level in a kind of inter-worldly resonance, as in the case of inter-body resonance on the physical level, since in the exchange with the "world" and life the inner connection becomes so strong that a common level could be reached. This is usually not noticeable, only the results show up in a kind of feedback - or "worldly response to life".

In practice and in everyday life, if you use the means of communication and formulate suitable phrases that describe a new attitude as it should be, you would have taken the right turn from the start, if you would have described it with adjectives that promote emotions, in this way you would create an inter-worldly resonance with your own life, which could reflect its echo back to the person. Then people are not only in relationships with people around them, such as family, friends, etc. - people would also be in relationships with the world as a whole and could allow communication to take effect, reflecting life in the form of results, events, coincidences and external happenings that fit with what the person had previously formulated.

Who says that we can only have one relationship with other people? We can establish relationships with animals, plants, things, plans, we establish relationships with places, memories, yes, we can even establish relationships with cars or motorbikes. And why then should we not have a relationship with life itself, which has created us as a miracle and lets us wake up anew every day, why should we not be able to communicate with it and expect the best that is already present in life, otherwise we would not be able to long for it. When life listens to us, we should resonate and express to it what is important to us - by admitting it to ourselves, because who is life if not ourselves?

I Talk; therefore, I Create

The "One-Phrase Method"

The incredibly useful learning competence of the brain helps us not to have to relearn actions that we perform repeatedly every time, but to be able to access the corresponding memory when needed. So, we don't have to use our thinking apparatus again and again or carry notes with us for everything we use in everyday life.

Be it the remembered route to work, the parents' phone number, the password for the e-mail program or the PIN number of the credit card - what the brain considers important is stored in the corresponding area. The motor cortex, for example, contains the learned ability to walk, swim or ride a bicycle, while the language center contains the learned languages, whereby each language has its own area. And when we formulate sentences that concern our goals, then we consciously or unconsciously give life the command to realize these goals in the environment due to constant repetitions of leading words and sentences. There is no one place where memory is located – on the contrary, our brain is permeated with memory content, just where the appropriate area lies. And since every person is individual, the personal learning portfolio, i.e. the combination of what one has learned so far in life, can also be considered unique in this compilation.

Theories of Reality by Prominent Scientists

It also results in the overall picture of a person, the construction of an ego, because after all, every person has different preferences for the content learned. This means that there are countless identities, personalities and again and again very individual constructs of reality, because everyone lives with his learned contents in a widely considered "self-made" world, which is based on experiences.

We do not decide in which family we are born, in which country we will be born, rich or poor, but we have the decision-making power to intervene in the directions of development of our further course of life and where we want to go, be, live and breathe.

Historical representatives of a *Radical Constructivism*, i.e. scientists such as the German epistemologist Ernst von Glasersfeld, the Viennese physicist and cyberneticist Heinz Foerster, or the neurobiologists Humberto R. Maturana and Francisco Valera, have long assumed that, roughly speaking, man can see nothing but self-constructed reality and that there is no world except the one, that you see and in which you live. The communication scientist Paul Watzlawick also postulated a connection to the outside world based purely on communication. But a lot of scientific criticism of this assumption could doubt the theses, so that according to the current state of affairs, it is assumed that the focus is on one's own "world" (with all that is relevant for the individual himself), but one can still perceive "the world of others".

When someone says:
"Just put yourself in his/her/my shoes!",

...the change of perspective may seem strange and unfamiliar at first, but it is still possible with a conscious intention. Therefore, "Constructivism" is not radical, i.e. people are completely focused on their own world, but one is also able, at least for a short time, to walk in the "shoes of others" and develop a certain understanding that also includes other ways of looking at things.

Changing the Way You View Reality

As part of the *One-Sentence Method*, you become aware of your own beliefs that have guided you in one direction or another in certain phases of life and then set about changing you so that new directions in life become possible. You overwrite old memorized sentences with a new list of phrases and repeat them daily to integrate them into your own self-image and to change and/or improve it. The emotionality in connection with the new affirmations creates contact from the inside to the outside and allows people, things and situations to move into the focus of the individual.

If, for example, you have never crocheted knitted hats, you will not notice the appropriate shops, objects and equipment. If you start to take a passionate interest in this new activity, a world with suitable content opens up for you. You now meet like-minded people, the places and opportunities become visible. As if they had been invisible before, you now find the connection to them, because everything is on the same wavelength.

Of course, these impressions already existed before, but you were blind to the things you had no connection with. The more you repeat the phrases and feel the emotion behind them ("...I am very happy about so many great opportunities, people and ideas to be able to pursue my new hobby (crocheting, knitting, football, singing, dancing, etc. ... !"), the more everything that is related to these phrases falls into the new perspective - as if it had always been there. And actually – it did!

Anyone who stops repeating things quickly falls back into old patterns and thus remains "loyal" to their usual identity and, as a result, to their usual life, even if they wanted to distance themselves from it. Discipline and perseverance are therefore essential until the new *engrams* (memory paths) have become second nature, and they no longer need to be practiced.

Thought Repetition Improves Sleep

The approach should not be confused with *Imagery Rehearsal Therapy* (IRT), which was developed specifically for the area of nightmares and can have demonstrable influences on a positively changed dream event by deliberately redesigning the sequence of the tormenting dream and repeating new images. According to the view of the Austrian psychoanalyst Sigmund Freud at the time, we are therefore the product of our previous experience, whereby, in his opinion, early childhood (first 3 years) is crucial. At the same time, unconscious family influences through communication patterns led to the development of depression and obsessive-compulsive disorders. However, numerous studies that follow people's personality development over the years confirm that personal identity is in flux throughout childhood and adolescence. Only then does it gradually solidify. However, we now know that upheavals are still possible even in older adulthood.

"We Are Shaped", ...but What Exactly Does that Mean?

Memory imprinting is a control center - it controls personal behavior: a collection of habits, created from origin and environment, controls the characteristics of people. If you change beliefs, the interpretation of environmental impressions changes, you see things "differently" and direct your attention accordingly to the focused impressions of the reality in which you move. You create new emotional goals, which change your charisma, attraction and results. By living in your own useful world, you now align your life completely with it. The brain mainly filters the external impressions that reach the individual internal switching or filtering points via the sensory organs and are then disposed of or stored. We therefore pay attention to what is attractive, useful or usable according to our interpretation of the incoming impressions. Everything that the closest people, such as parents or other close relatives or later teachers and friends, said was stored as correct and important, even if there was a lot of "mental rubbish" in it.

What is stored was associated with a feeling, otherwise it would not have qualified for long-term storage. We often remember a toy that was important to us; it was probably highly emotional and is stored deep down so that it has not been forgotten even today. In this way, our subconscious guides us through everyday life and we go to places that are important according to our "construction", eating what we individually consider to be good and tasty.

If we did not like broccoli in childhood, even if it was good for us, we have stored our mother's warning together with the unpleasant taste and may feel guilty whenever broccoli is offered to us, but we politely decline. This is how we are conditioned. To become friends with broccoli now would mean we would have to overcome certain inner obstacles (more on this later in the chapter "The Crocodile Bridge"). If it is not important to us, and we cannot provide any emotions for it, broccoli will not be a topic on our dinner table in the future. So, if we repeatedly find ourselves in the wrong relationships, jobs, situations, financial difficulties or other recurring problems, it probably has something to do with how we have learned to behave and make decisions in these areas. We can relearn so that all areas of our lives can benefit and improve.

A direct connection between the brain/subconscious, body and the outside world attracts people, things, places and situations that we are consciously or unconsciously focused on. In earlier times, it was reserved for hypnotists or psychotherapists to instill new insights, guidelines, ideals and instructions into people in meditative or hypnotized states via faster access to the subconscious. Today we can make these inner changes ourselves if we design new learning processes and allow them to seep into the subconscious through regular repetition, from where they can connect with the outside world and have an effect.

The 1st Law

The Transformation Should Be
Clearly Thought Out and Formulated

You are born perfect, but then you are "educated".

Beliefs, opinions, attitudes, prejudices, principles, and wisdom from others are then channeled into your brain via your sensory organs and burned into your memory through repetition as engrams (mental inscriptions). These engrams are now your signposts, the individual mental routes of your "life plan" made by others, which unconsciously show you the direction.

Every day you now think, speak and act according to these guidelines. But there is the part of you that feels external control and is sometimes not happy with it. In addition, the results of your being the way you are show themselves on the outside - people, things and situations show the effects of an upbringing that you did not choose yourself. One part of you wants change, the other part is afraid of it, because the long-repeated behaviors that have become habits are not so easy to break. The brain loves its routine, and deviations create fear and uncertainty.

But who is in charge here? Is it our own brain or is it fate that treats us either well or badly? Are we self-determined or are we determined by others? Who determines our life and our path? Me? You? Someone else? Something else? God? Or am I, are you God in our own life? What role does the brain play in the question of how our life develops, happiness, success, reputation and career - is all of this determined, or do we have a say in it? If so, how much? Or is everything completely in our hands and are we completely self-sufficient and independent?

Whenever people cannot explain a situation, they look for the solution in mysticism, the inexplicable, the supernatural. What if everything is controlled by us?

In the religious beliefs of Christianity and Islam, the idea of fate is synonymous with paying homage to a God who has predetermined everything for all people from the very beginning.

"It is not I who determine my life, but you..." and "...just say the word and my soul will be healed" are sayings from the Bible that express and demand complete devotion to a higher power. People then accept that life, as it is, has something to do with providence and that they must fit in with it - and not even try to go in other directions.

Who knows exactly how much power we really have in our own lives?

Determinism:

The belief in fate is often embedded or shaped in religion. The assumption that the fate of man is in the hands of God or an overpowering divine being - belief in divine providence, which plays an important role in Islam and Christianity. Augustine of Hippo and Martin Luther taught that divine grace is the only thing that works, and that man is incapable of earning salvation through good works.

Everything is predetermined - this rules out the existence of free will decisions and thus certain actions from the outset. It sees the pursuit of self-determination and changing the world as an illusion.

Causal determinism:

This way of thinking assumes that everything is a consequence of one's own actions. Karma concepts attribute a significant influence on the future to human decisions. Fate is the influence on a person's life that is, however, beyond his control. The idea of fate is older than philosophy. The Greek epic poets and dramatists formulated fate as blind power or as a lot, the early natural philosophers (Thales, Anaximander, Heraclitus and others) understood natural laws as fate.

From a religious point of view, the concept of fate is transformed into the concept of divine predestination (predetermination), from a scientific point of view, the concept of determination (determination) takes the place of fate, without this disappearing as a subjective experience. The theme of fate essentially and independently of the specific terminology is the intertwining of self-determination and external determination.

These are two extreme directions: Either all fate is in the sense of external determination and man is thus also exempt from responsibility, or fate is the unrecognized but natural consequence of individual actions and views, and is therefore not an enemy, but a logical result of one's own actions. Someone who is born into certain circumstances develops differently than if he/she had been born into other circumstances.

The environment shapes people with his convictions, morals and beliefs, which, in addition to genetic dispositions, make him what he later becomes. Phrases such as "You can do this/you can't do that" or "That's the way/that's not the way" flow into the deepest layers of the brain and remain there in the memory, possibly forever, influencing and deciding on success and failure, marriage or eternal singleness, etc.

"My brain is the master of life.
It, or I myself, decide where I'm going!"

"Every connection to the outside world brings me
the greatest possible success and experiences
that are to my benefit!"

To regain control, you have to change the sentences that shape your life and, through practice, establish new or expanded beliefs that will one day override the automatism of the old beliefs. If a person deviates from this and wants to believe and live something else, such as "I can do it!", fears and doubts quickly arise, a "crocodile bridge" opens up, so to speak, that one must cross. New affirmations penetrate the deepest layers of memory through constant repetition and provide new control. The personality is defined by previous instructions from parents and the environment and largely identifies with the content of the upbringing that was conveyed, which now leads a life of its own through regular repetition.

"You can't do this; you can't do that."

New phrases cause the integrated beliefs to falter, and insecurity arises because the brain loses its usual framework, its identity, which is fed by phrases that were learned early on. Because even if the learned beliefs and prejudices (including about oneself) are negative and self-damaging, one holds on to them, because the brain loves routine, even if it is negative, the main thing is familiar territory, feeling at home, no matter what.

How do you find out how you can integrate new, positive things into the depths of your brain and overcome the fears that come with them? The answer lies in the daily repetition of new, better beliefs that not only change and reshape your identity but also steer your whole life in new directions. In this way, the mind directs exactly what people previously thought was their unalterable fate. I am not saying that there is no such thing as fate and that people can control everything. Nobody knows exactly what forces are at work between heaven and earth.

What Fires Together, Wires Together.

From a neurophysiological point of view, learning can be understood as the formation of synaptic connections. The more often neurons are active at the same time, the more likely they are to connect with each other. The ability of the nervous system to reorganize itself plays a fundamental role in learning and storing memory content as well as in recovering from cerebral damage. Experience is therefore the repository for the events, situations and learning units that have shaped our personality. Experience thus serves the brain as an orientation tool to read the future, which then becomes a loop of repetition of the past due to the same behavior. Old experiences thus become new plans.

If you want to achieve change, you should be very attentive and no longer act according to old experiences, which in some cases still make sense, but are sometimes only repeat offenders in a damaging way. One famous follower of *Radical Constructivism*,

Ernst von Glasersfeld, described very impressively that we abstract our knowledge from what we have experienced so far and thus build it ourselves - similar *"to a physical skill":*

"The thinking subject can only construct its knowledge on the basis of its experience."

"What we make of our experience forms the world in which we consciously live." (v. Glasersfeld, 1995)

If all people live in worlds based on experience and constructed accordingly, this also means that we evaluate circumstances differently depending on what we`ve learned and seen in the past. This logically leads to misunderstandings and disagreements among people, as our respective foundations are naturally different, and our experiences also differ from one another. The Marburg philosopher and biologist Gerhard Roth added that the brain creates *real reality* from three areas:

• External world
• Physical world
• Self-world (mental and emotional states)

The *external world* and the *physical world* differ from one another, but the *self-world* and the *physical world* can hardly be separated from one another. The other people, things and places are therefore on the outside, but me and my body are in direct relation to myself. The connection that one has with oneself and with the people and things plays an important role in the personal development and goal achievement of the individual.

If I am in trouble with my environment, no great success can be expected here, whether professionally or privately. If body and mind are in harmony, this is reflected in the personal environment, because the environment shows a person as a reflection of their inner state, so working on oneself is essential if one wants to be successful on the outside.

A Magical Connection-
Brain, Body and Environment

Emotions allow you to get on the same wavelength as your environment. There are waves such as acoustic sound waves, of which the ear can only perceive 16 to 20,000 heart frequencies, or electromagnetic waves of light, which the eye can see as violet or red light. When you stand opposite a person, you can quickly sense through their charisma, impression and shared chemistry whether you are on the same wavelength. If you greet someone warmly, you usually get a corresponding response. If you treat yourself well, life usually reacts accordingly via the internal connections of a *brain-body-environmental axis.*

If you think positively, the brain releases positive hormones that help, for example, to speed up the healing process when you are not feeling well physically. If you tell yourself what you need and back it up with positive emotions, life will reflect your goal to you and you will experience it, provided your relationship with it is pleasant and relaxed. Emotional tension produces the same thing in reverse, so that the goal moves further away.

Everything we are, everything we have achieved, is based on decisions that we have made based on feelings. Even the decisions that are supposedly guided by reason are the result of a previous weighing up of pros and cons, in which feelings initially played a role and then made the choice for the "sensible" solution. Feelings, in turn, arise from thoughts and inner attitudes.

Experiment: Think for 2 minutes about all the people in your life who have said or done *bad things* to you.

The release of the corresponding hormones then creates *bad feelings.*

A bad feeling is the result of a hormone release that negatively affects both the mind and the body. The best-known hormones that the body releases during a stress reaction are noradrenaline, adrenaline and cortisol. Noradrenaline and adrenaline belong to the so-called sympathoadrenomedullary system (SAM - important subsystem of the sympathetic nervous system and central component of the fight-or-flight response, in which sym-pathetic nerves innervate the adrenal medulla, where they stim-ulate the release of adrenaline and noradrenaline, among other things). This system is activated immediately when a person is exposed to a stress factor.

The situation is different when you think of people or situations in which something good happened to you, someone said some-thing nice to you and this triggered happy feelings. Here, hor-mones or neurotransmitters are activated that can cause feelings of well-being or happiness. The best known are dopamine, sero-tonin and endorphin. Others are called noradrenaline, phenethyl-amine and oxytocin. It is important to realize that once you are aware of this, you can learn to control and manage your own feel-ings. It all depends on what you focus on in your mind:

I remember once being so upset about a canceled date that my anger lasted for quite some time. Every day I was internally upset about the person in question, my negative thoughts turned into unpleasant feelings that accompanied me almost all day. After five days had passed, I realized that my anger was of no use to me at all. And so, I decided to just let the anger be. I turned off the feeling through a decision of will and at the same time was amazed at how easy it was to do this. Feelings dictate which direction we go, which plan we follow and which we don't. Every piece of furniture in your home, every friendship, a move to a foreign country, whether it's the desire to have children or the choice of a certain salad dressing, everything you have, are and will be, determined by a previous feeling. You could say that your feelings rule the world you live in. And your feelings are just as much as the rulers of the life that you will lead in the future.

Everything begins with the word. Because the word, the thought triggers the feeling.

Exercise: Repeat desired words/beliefs in the now form. Repetition is the key.

*"The people around me **ARE** reliable,*
I like to meet reliable people."

You create new impressions by formulating and repeating desired behaviors and characteristics of others. The brain then focuses on exactly this type of person, and you overlay old word impressions that have always led you in the same direction of type of person.

Decide for yourself today what kind of company you want and whether you no longer want to experience old, harmful patterns in your contacts.

How do I recognize my current feelings? When it comes to money? Relationship? Love? Is there enough of everything or is there a shortage? Do I meet people who are not trustworthy? Do I give too much? With my willingness to give, do I attract precisely those who are out to enrich themselves at the expense of others?

If I am annoyed by the untidy way a colleague works, there will certainly be a corresponding counterpart within myself, otherwise I would not be interested in the topic at all. Maybe I do not allow myself to be a little careless now and then, do not allow myself a break or vacation and feel provoked by the relaxed attitude of others, the unconscious part of me signals:

"Give yourself a little peace and quiet too."

Making mistakes sometimes is not so bad. If you recognize this, you don't experience your colleague as a disturbing subject, but as a real messenger of important information about yourself that helps to improve life on certain levels. If you walk through the world smiling, the world can't help but smile back. You experience the same mirror effect when you have a grim expression.

My World, Your World - Our World

Everything that is relevant in any way comes to people via invisible sources, streams and frequencies. Everything is connected. People meet their own kind. When they change their nature, their beliefs and their imprints, they find themselves in a new world with other people around them. People who are afraid of commitment meet what they themselves are without knowing it. Perhaps the expression is less pronounced in them, and they therefore feel less restricted. Then they fight for the other person's willingness to have a relationship, not realizing that as soon as the other person gets involved, their own fears will come to the fore even more and they will take on the role of the avoidant partner. An uncomfortable oscillation between closeness and distance only ends when one of the two gets out of it and becomes authentic.

In a study by New York's Columbia University, researchers had people pray for 219 women with unfulfilled desire to have children. Fertility is said to have improved noticeably as a result. In this study, neither the patients nor the doctors treating them knew anything about the intercessions. Harold Koenig, director of the Center for Religious, Spiritual and Health Studies at Duke University in North Carolina, USA, is nevertheless convinced of the stress-reducing effect of personal prayer. The immune, hormonal and circulatory systems are activated by the positive thinking and trust shown in prayer and promote a relaxed attitude that is beneficial to health. Such results can generally be achieved with a positive attitude to life. Neurotransmitters in the brain, such as serotonin, which promotes well-being, are always released when you relax. Seen in this way, prayer is a variant of autosuggestion. Despite the observation of our own, individual world in which everyone lives, we are not included in it, otherwise we would never be able to watch a concert together, watch a movie together and discuss it, or get advice about a particular product in a shop.

The Munich psychiatrist and philosopher Thomas Fuchs describes the existence of a shared *intersubjective space* that we enter when we meet others. Exchange takes place through language, through acoustic waves, haptic communication through the skin through touch. If we lived purely in our own world, exchange with an environment would not be possible at all. The brain itself can only act in symbiosis with the body; if you put it in a glass of nutrient solution, this disembodied brain would not be able to perceive the brain-body-environmental connection neces-sary for interaction with the outside world. The exchange with the world and people would fail, because without a functioning "body apparatus" and the necessary interaction with it, it would be merely a solo organism preoccupied with itself and its subjective world. Of course, we perceive the world from our own perspec-tive, but it is not an illusion of the mind, but part of a shared reality in which we exchange common impressions and experience things. Fuchs also speaks of the existence of a *social self* that interacts with other people and the *ecological self* that cultivates exchange with the environment and nature. At this point I would add an *economic self*, an inner entity that is connected to topics such as economic interests.

"It's great to have and keep money."

If this ego is restricted in any way, the areas mentioned above suffer. For example, there is frequent, temporary or permanent unemployment, economic debt and other related economic is-sues that can worsen the life of the person affected. Improvement can occur if this economic ego changes its identification with the previously false beliefs (e.g. "Rich people are bad, arrogant and lacking in empathy!"), weakens and reduces them by consistently implicating new identifications.

The Filter of Selective Perception

We see what we want to see or already expect. The inner filter of selective attention is therefore always oriented towards the life story of the individual. As Thorsten Fehr from the Institute for Brain Research at the University of Bremen explains, this is also expressed in selective perception, in the fact that environmental stimuli or parts of reality are given particular attention.

Psychology professor Daniel Simons' "Gorilla Experiment" is one of the best-known tests for selective perception today. The participants watched a video of two teams playing ball and were asked to count how often the ball went back and forth. But because everyone was so focused on the ball, they overlooked the person who ran through the field for minutes dressed as a gorilla.

The Bremen scientist gives the following example: If a driver drives through a residential area during the day, he expects that small children could run into the street. However, if he is driving through the same area in the middle of the night, he does not expect this. His attention is different - and with it what he perceives of his environment. Fehr assumes that people develop a kind of filter based on their learning history. However, there are large individual differences. This means that for some people, the image they have of reality is closer to the actual situation than for others. One of the findings that researchers have gained in recent years, he says, is that selective perception becomes less important as people get older. Older people have a good eye for visible reality.

What Is *Subjective* and *Selective* Perception?

Selective perception is a "judgment error" in which our brain unconsciously filters sensory impressions and blocks out information. The reason for this is limited attention or deliberately directed perception. A simple example: the nose is constantly in our field of vision - but we still don't see it because the brain considers it to be "unimportant" now and simply blocks it out. What we put on in the morning, our clothes, we don't see during the day, we don't pay attention to it because it was checked off as OK in the morning, there is no longer any need for us to concern ourselves with it.

Subjective and selective perception are synonyms - the two cannot be separated from one another: our perception is always shaped and influenced by our own personality, experiences, expectations and emotions. Selected information is interpreted subjectively and then treated as facts, although it is only a fragment of reality.

Why Is Perception Subjective and Selective?

Every second, people perceive thousands of impressions through their senses. It would be impossible to process all of them. The brain must select to cope with the flood of information. In doing so, it adapts our perception to the respective context and the current emotional state. Criticism and insults are particularly likely to remain in the subconscious, as the brain wants to heal and thoughts therefore revolve around negative things for longer, i.e. to process problematic events.

How can you know where you are in life, what you have achieved and what significance that has if we do not measure ourselves against other people? We all have a need for self-evaluation. *"What am I like, what was I like, how did I manage this and that?*

What does it say about me? What do I offer, what can I do?" - and so on.

Within the "Theory of Social Comparisons", which the social psychologist Leon Festinger described in 1954, upward comparisons can make us feel bad because looking up to the higher status of others creates a feeling of worthlessness. On the other hand, if we compare ourselves downwards with others, we feel better because we are looking down on those who have achieved less in life than ourselves. However, the comparison is only emotionally painful if it is directed upwards. Comparing ourselves with others is important so that we can see where we stand in life.

Sandy Müller is a very helpful woman who is always there for everyone and never turns down a favor. She should be liked by many people, but the opposite is the case. She lives in a three-story apartment building without an elevator and very often accepts packages for her neighbors. When the delivery person rings her doorbell, she immediately offers to let him leave all the packages with her so that he does not have to climb the stairs to the neighbors. But then the neighbors upstairs must pick up the packages, that would otherwise have been delivered to their apartment door, from Mrs. Müller on the ground floor and carry them up by themselves.

So, Mrs. Müller`s excessive willingness to help favors some of the people but disadvantages others, which leads to rejections of her. The mirrored information shows, however, based on the results of her behavior, where she is acting too extremely, so that it is disturbing to some of the people around her.

She could ask herself how to improve the results in her relationships, contacts and friendships through targeted self-change. People around us and especially the relationships we enter open up important messages for us.

By recognizing ourselves in them, by reflecting our behavior in their behavior, we see the truth about ourselves, we become aware of our strengths and weaknesses, we find out what may be wrong with us. From these contacts we get exactly the information we need to be able to change. Let's look at the results of the friendships and relationships we have. From this we can see whether we have formulated the right or the wrong life sentences.

Here are two example mantras, memorized and often repeated, mostly learned from people we care about or adopted from others who we thought always had the right words to say.

"I have to give everything to others!"

"I have no time for myself!"

And again, these words act as a route planner and describe the path to more of these life plans, to more disadvantages in life, which, due to their repetition and the never-ending belief in them, reproduce repeatedly, with all the misfortune that comes with it. You always can change your mantras.

A new world opens when you are ready to exchange the old one for a better one.

Controlling Your Body's Hormones
with Words

Our inner self, what we think and feel, is in constant social inter-action with our external world. This happens not only through ver-bal communication such as the exchange of words, but also through non-verbal communication such as looks, facial expres-sions, gestures, hearing and smells. For example, sweat is se-creted through our skin, which can be perceived by others in our environment. Feelings of fear and expressions of dominance are also transported outwards via these channels and give the world in which we live an impression of who we are, how we see our-selves and how we are feeling now.

If we were completely focused on ourselves, external influences would have little effect on us. As social beings, however, we can only turn away from what is happening outside of ourselves temporarily. We naturally stay in contact again and again. Social influences from outside have an impact on how we think and feel - and thus also on our hormone levels.

Communication Can Be Good or Bad for the Body

So, if someone says something bad, the effect will be negative in most cases. We don't feel good; the opinions of others sometimes touch us deeply and it bothers us. We are not as resilient as we would like to be. The words, comments, opinions of the people around us influence our hormone balance, they stress us, trigger surges that can either be positive, like when we receive compliments and happiness hormones like serotonin or dopamine are released, or we feel stressed, so that a signal is sent to the brain to immediately flood the body with cortisol and adrenaline or other substances, for example, and thus set a direction. Women after the menopause can sometimes be heard saying:

"I don't need a man anymore, I don't want to get to know anyone, I'm no longer interested, I don't attach any importance to it anymore." Perhaps the motivation to get involved in relationships has weakened for hormonal reasons and also due to experience, but if you think and say the sentences just mentioned, this motivation does not increase but rather decreases. You tell yourself that your best days are over, and then it surely will happen as you said it.

Consciously Create Neuronal Changes

Things develop differently, however, if you say: "Getting older, so what? What does that mean? I want to continue to enjoy my life, and I am not going to hide behind the stove like an old cat. In addition to work and obligations, life should also bring fun and good humor - if I get to know someone, then that's how it is and I'm happy about it."

With these positive views, you shape and code your own subconscious and the appropriate influences from outside can reach the person, just like with the view that you have nothing more to expect in this life - this is also imprinting and coding and influences on what's coming up to you from the outside world. The image that it provides then reflects what you said to yourself. So why not say and express what brings the maximum benefit to the person?

The American psychologists Meyer and Seligman were among the scientists who discovered, from a neuroplastic perspective, that the brain creates new neural connections due to repeated words and sentences - ones that can overlay old connections. According to medical studies, pessimistic views are also as harmful as 2.5 packs of cigarettes and contribute to an increased risk of heart attack. Seligman recommended that psychology should focus less on poking around in the disorders and instead develop more positive perspectives for the individual. Because continuing to deal with negativity, even if it serves the purpose of healing it, keeps the thinker on a dark, damaging, mental level - hardly conducive to the goal of wanting to free oneself from it.

But not all hormones are produced in the brain. Our supplier of feelings of happiness, serotonin, for example, produces 95% of it in the intestine. The medical authors, Burkhardt and Neubauer report that signals are transmitted directly to the brain via a gut-brain axis, i.e. the gut can control our feelings as if it were a kind of "second brain". Nutrition also plays an important role when it comes to influencing our feelings positively or, in the worst case, negatively. Hormones control our feelings and thus ultimately also what we say - to ourselves and to others. Since this is the case, it must also be possible for our words to control how we feel and what emotional influence we have on others through communication in a kind of feedback loop.

How Words Control Your Own Environment

Our hormones, regulated by different sides and influences, can ensure that we feel good or bad and that we react positively or negatively to our environment accordingly - then words that initially arise from our thoughts can also control us and our environment. So, if you consciously say something positive to yourself and to others, it has a positive influence on yourself and on other people, depending on who the positive words are directed at. In conclusion, the positive word influences the body's own hormones, which help control emotions, thoughts and behavior. The same applies in the negative case. This allows us to conclude that by using the right words we can direct our hormones in the direction we want.

Situations are what they are - if we evaluate them as good or bad, depending on our own conditioning, the appropriate hormone release follows. If we change our interpretations, the way our body reacts to the changed state of mind also changes - how it regulates the respective hormones. Words and thoughts can contribute to both physical well-being and illness. They sometimes work like medicine that can either heal or be toxic, depending on how the person perceives them in accordance with their personality DNA.

It is therefore not sensible to say to yourself in old age: "The shine is off," because this can lead to the shine coming off indeed and you feel worse, devalued and tired instead of fitter, more energetic and more motivated, which you could have achieved with a more positive self-description. It is better to use the right words to guide your body and hormones where you want them to be - towards happiness, well-being and goal achievement.

"I am happy every day that I have great potential for strength, energy and stamina!"

The brain is open to learning processes, even if it initially clings to old routines out of habit. The more often you say this sentence or similar sentences to yourself, the faster your brain will turn your goal into reality. Our own way of thinking determines which hormones our body releases and which it doesn't. If we spend the whole day thinking negatively, we're not doing ourselves any favors.

Often, however, this way of thinking doesn't come from malice towards our environment but can be an automatic process that has arisen out of habit and that we can't easily turn off. We must be careful, because if we indulge in criticism and negativity, we are also constantly living with stress hormones that are damaging to us. Our charisma changes, other people turn away because they get the feeling that we're not a good place to be.

The Brain as a Prediction Machine

Are You Living the Life You Are Used to Or the Life You Want?

If you believe in a theory of fate, the destiny of everyone is decided by the whim of a providence that brings people into this world rich or poor, in war or in peace, healthy or sick, privileged or disadvantaged. Many believe that this firm providence decides how we should live, because our abilities, and thus our origins, were already instilled in us at birth.

Genes determine the direction, but many external influences on which people are subject in the course of their lives shape and, under certain circumstances, lead in directions that we would not have thought possible due to our own socialization. The phrase "from rags to riches" is a synonym for the possibility of being able to achieve (almost) anything in life despite any origin. Then the question arises: "How did he/she do it?" From simple or very simple circumstances to big money, success, respect, recognition and more? How can that be possible?

The human brain adjusts to expected events based on previous experiences to be able to control the future. If you want to have new, different and better experiences, it is necessary to place new *engrams* (brain pathways) to give the mind a vision of what is imaginable (and thus implementable) in the future and subsequently achievable. And so, it adjusts to the new, the person has now planned and looked ahead to his or her future life through thoughts that have become habitual in thinking, and not an external world. There are countless such stories, biographies with unexpected breaks in unexpected new directions. It seems that people can influence things and thus take matters into their own hands based on certain behaviors.

Why is it difficult at first to decide on a path that you really want from the bottom of your heart? And why do the feelings that you once developed for your previous life often get in the way when you set your sights on something new? What role do feelings play in this context? Torn between old and new perspectives words, affirmations trigger feelings -> feelings trigger new worlds. The brain orientates itself on its own, previous experiences and predicts the future from this source. The fear of "hand on the hot stove" - you experience it once and from then on you are cautious and have learned not to endanger yourself. When you approach a source of danger, you first weigh up how to deal with it. Here we are dealing with a useful protective function that leads to you not taking too great risks. Negative interpersonal experiences can lead to the realization:

"All people are bad!"

...but at the same time, it also triggers you to look after yourself on the one hand, but at the same time to close yourself off from people. Here we are dealing with a not very useful but very protective function that, if you live it in an exaggerated form, leads to isolation. It would be more helpful to create a new sentence that you say to yourself every day so that it can constantly seep into your own subconscious. Because just as you go through life with the coloring of your own conditioning, you will always meet exactly the people who fit that conditioning.

"I'm just so glad that I have very kind,
reliable friends who I value very much."

...leads to more of what you have formulated in the phrase, because charisma, decisiveness and friendliness change insofar as you feel it inside. In the long run, it is difficult to pretend. In fact, there is a danger of having bad experiences with people whenever you want and need something from them, give up too much of yourself in the process or give more than you get back. A possible engram based on a false insight or upbringing could be:

"I have to give a lot to be loved.
Being is not enough."

But then you continue to live the old pattern and keep getting exactly what you don't want: ignorance, neglect, exploitation, abuse. And this basically repeats everything that you had to experience in childhood. How about a slightly different engram here:

"People love me the way I am.
I don't have to do anything for it. Being is enough."

The sentence becomes ingrained through daily repetition, and you say it to yourself until you see the first external results - and you should keep saying the sentence even after that, otherwise old patterns can creep back in.

You can tell from the external results whether you have relapsed, because living out old patterns is a secret addiction of the brain, as it is in patterns, routines and habits. New things generate rejection, which can even be felt physically (more on this in the chapter: *"Crocodile Bridge"*). The old beliefs were imprinted at some point in the past, probably by people you cared about in your childhood (e.g. a demanding, never satisfied mother). You then no longer dare to be yourself and believe that you always must function to receive affection and attention. This opens the door to exploitative people.

"I am loved unconditionally.
I now receive unlimited affection and love.
I am enough with everything that I am now."

Solution: Place a new engram and memorize it every day to weaken the old belief and allow the new one to become more dominant. Because what is repeated has greater power and shows the brain a prediction for a better future, better contacts and opportunities and overwrites or weakens the old "predictions". The longer you hold on to it, the more you see external results that emerge over time.

Then the brain no longer feeds itself from the past with old sentences like:

**"I am not good enough; I must do something to get love
and attention. I must bend and pretend,
I must not be myself."**

The brain relates words directly to itself, so self-created constructions work best and most intensively.

Someone gives you a compliment and then you feel good, if you hear insulting words, you feel bad afterwards. I relate it to myself. When I say good words to myself, I feel good, then the external equivalents are triggered that match feelings. If you are repeatedly exploited by others and are surprised because you have given so much and expected gratitude or at least appreciation and honesty, then you should ask yourself why you always give so much. Isn't that also a type of exploitation, albeit unconsciously, to think that the more I give, the more I must be given back? Maybe the person I'm talking to doesn't want to get that much and at the same time decides for themselves how much they are prepared to invest in this friendship, this contact, this relationship.

Some marriages were formed out of pure gratitude. One person did a lot for the other and when the other person thought at some point, perhaps in old age, that there were probably no more options, they got married and showed their gratitude. The years of support from a partner who was waiting longingly for the other's open heart and was now finally to be rewarded was honored in this way. But is that the kind of love we want? Let's not wait for others to give us their good gifts, words and attention. Let's use the right words to plan a life that is carried by love and creates a future with positivity that is based above all on our own stable independence, which we plant in our minds again and again every day until we see it on the outside.

Words become a daily experience, and the brain creates a vision for the future from them. Open, direct paths as well as indirect, hidden paths that are imperceptible to the human senses and exist via an inner world-outer world connection lead us in the direction that we have set this time and, in a mirror reaction, bring everything that we have already planted inside us onto our path. Up until now, we have encountered what others have planted in us. The brain does not decide which plant is good or bad but takes and carries out what is there. Our task now is to plant the garden in the way that we want to see the seeds next spring.

Speaking in the Superlative

How Small Sentences Create Great Things

Why should we not be entitled to the best of everything? If there are people who can buy communication platforms for billions and others eagerly await their paycheck at the end of the month so that they can even buy food, why is that? If some people fly into space at their own expense and others don't have the money to have their shoes resoled, how is that possible?

The way both groups of people think and feel is fundamentally different, and this book is about how we can use the connections between the body, environment, thoughts and feelings to create a harmonious unity of these elements through language, which takes us to the right places, the right people and the fulfillment of our goals at the right time. No one becomes rich in life if he or she doesn't think in broader terms. When I talk to financially disadvantaged people about their situation, I often hear an attitude that is not characterized by abundance and a belief in big capital. You find yourself in a cycle of laboriously earning your monthly salary, paying bills and considering when and whether things will ever get better financially in the future. You never have the secure feeling that there is enough of everything, even though that is exactly the reality. In this unpleasant cycle, which repeats the same old scenario every month, there is no room for change, because old thinking and feeling creates the same old life, characterized by familiar situations that you conjure up again month after month with your own inner conviction.

Changing the way you communicate internally, even if only playfully at first, with yourself and the environment, would result in visibly changed situations. Thinking playfully in large categories and giving in to the feelings that arise from this can create something new on the outside - but at this point people give in again, understandably, because unknown areas are initially frightening - you don't know exactly what will happen.

Phrases like: *"You have to be content."* - lead to having enough reasons to perceive life as mediocre. *"I am absolutely happy that I am entitled to the best and that I receive the fullness of life every day!"*

...leads to people, places and situations that reflect this in the same way. We were not raised to think and speak highly of ourselves. In truth, we feel ashamed when we are praised, we downplay it, because for a long time this behavior was considered a virtue. And if someone boasted about his or her achievements, we became suspicious because we had learned that this was not appropriate. We act modestly so that people like us and do not think badly of us.

Let's Try to Think and Speak in Superlatives, Even If it Feels Strange.

Everyone has a need for acceptance by their fellow human beings. But the price we pay for this is sometimes high. If modest thinking and feeling contributes to a modest life and cautious thinking and feeling means giving up opportunities, then failures and, consequently, an empty bank account are no surprise. After all, a life that includes all the goals we really strive for is also strange and new at first.

If we want things to be different, we must be prepared to accept the other and at least open a small door inside for it.

Good - Better - Best

Thinking bigger, positive adjectives, acting bigger achieves the fulfillment of bigger goals if we are prepared to do so without apologizing for it.

"I don't want a better job, that would be the comparison to other jobs. I want the best job, number 1."

"I don't want nicer friends, nicer than those I knew, but the nicest friends."

"I don't want to be able to cope with everything financially more easily, but I want this area to be the easiest."

It's no use telling someone that you want it that way for yourself, you have to say it to yourself, because then you're telling it to life - which in turn reacts to it and presents the people who have the best and most decent behavior as an echo. The best cannot appear if it has no value in your own language, because only that which is already perceived and practiced as normal in your own thinking and in everyday formulation is accepted.

The most beautiful, the biggest, the fastest, the most efficient and so on sounds at first like boasting or like a glutton. But this is only a question of perspective. People who are bothered by big thinking and formulation, in favor of how others judge them, based on the successes they deserve in life. Some believe that demanding the least for themselves is a virtue and would lead to more acceptance and love. But people look at those who have achieved as much as possible in their lives, sometimes with envy, but more often with admiration. Who cares or takes as their role model those who, out of false modesty, never want anything for themselves?

Say:

"The problem has already been solved!" -

and so be it.

We all know it, a problem, an argument, a conflict, something stupid that someone said to us stays with us for hours, sometimes weeks - it often robs us of sleep. We keep thinking about something that may still be simmering under the surface but really should finally be put to rest.

But – we cannot let go, our brain wants to heal and therefore continues to focus on the issue, which now only has a gnawing and disturbing effect on our inner peace.

I remember that I was once quite annoyed because someone had cancelled a long-planned trip without further ado. The reasons given were not very credible and only made me more annoyed. So, I was angry for five days, I couldn't stop thinking about the impertinence and carried an unpleasant, burdening feeling with me the whole time. The matter was settled, but the inner hurt still needed a while to heal. Everything revolved around the experience and the thoughts could not be turned off. Then finally, after the five days mentioned, I thought to myself:

"Yes, the issue is annoying. But I don't feel like being angry anymore. I'll just stop. I'll let it go."

And the anger went away as soon as I decided to let it go. I finally wanted to feel normal again, to carry on living my life as before.

However, I was amazed at how easily you can control not only your thoughts, but also your feelings with your conscious will.

In another situation, a teacher had disagreements with the students in a class. After they had discussed the communication problem, things should have calmed down. But there was still a vague feeling of negativity in the air, the bad mood was still there.

Then one day the teacher said to himself:

"I don't feel like dealing with this issue anymore. I hereby declare the problem solved."

And whenever his mind tried to deal with this very issue again, he put it in its place by simply saying to himself again:

"The problem is already in the past. It no longer exists. It's been done for a long time."

When he came to the course the next time, the students expected a certain reaction from him, but he was no longer able to offer one, because for him the matter was done - simply because he had declared it done, after a solution had been found. There was nothing left to clarify, only the negative residual vibrations were still lingering, so that this could have been calmed down again through conversation.

His word, his decision, his unwillingness to think further about something that could easily have been enlarged, intensified and escalated - he dropped all of that and thus gave those around him no longer any point of attachment to continue to work on it. However, they expected that something else would have to come now, they had apparently not yet said goodbye to the problem.

So, the students assumed that he would say something about the matter, but he didn't and continued with his work as before. And the people around him took note of his behavior and did the same. They also let go of the problem, even though a few things could have been sorted out. But he showed no willingness to deal with it any further and for the others it was over. He had determined, through clear words - to himself - that the problem was solved, and with that it was also gone, because the world reacts to what we say to ourselves. It can be that simple when you take control of your life, change your thoughts, change your words, then come to different decisions, create a reflection of the outside world and shape your own reality in a way that you consider important and meaningful. You don't have to tell others what you expect, you should create something new within yourself and simply say goodbye to a problem that you want to get rid of from within yourself.

What needs to be clarified must be clarified and then decide that the problem is solved. It is different to sweep things under the rug, that is not what this means. Is there something to be clarified? Then clarify it and then stop - and above all, stop hating. It is done, you can let it go, the problem is already in the past, it doesn't even exist anymore.

Self-Fulfilling Prophecies

What you say to yourself every day becomes a habit, becomes a routine, becomes a personal truth. And everyone who lives his own truth and believes in it makes the decisions that fit it, leads the life that fits it.

How can the outside world do anything other than show through people, places and situations as a kind of a medium exactly what you live, think and internalize? Sentences become a *self-fulfilling prophecy*.

Famous examples such as the *Pygmalion Effect* show that positive statements can have a huge impact on the lives of individuals or entire groups.

The Pygmalion Effect:

The assumption and statement of a teacher in an American school that the students were all great, very intelligent and talented, although there was no evidence of this, led to the prophecy coming true at the end of the year and all students had achieved high performance and very good grades.

- Students whose teachers had positive expectations because of the supposedly better IQ test results developed better and reached their full potential.

- Students whose teachers had no expectations, on the other hand, performed worse.

This is also the case with the example of the **Rosenthal Effect** with students and a few rats:

Twelve students were each given five rats. Half of the students were told that their rats were particularly clever. The other half were told that their rats were extremely stupid. However, there was no difference between the animals. When the rats then had to go through a maze, it was shown that the clever rats found the exit faster than the stupid rats. The students' behavior towards their rats therefore influenced the rats' performance.

The **Rosenthal Effect**, like the **Pygmalion effect,** was able to prove that teachers' expectations can influence students' performance.

The **Placebo Effect** is also well known:

In medicine, belief in the effectiveness of a supposed drug leads to an actual improvement in health. Although the drug has no active ingredients, an effect can be achieved through expectation.

And then there is the **Corona Effect:**

The fear that there could be a shortage of toilet paper, and that people would no longer be able to clean themselves at a time when there is a particular focus on personal hygiene, especially because of the transmissibility of viruses. The fear of shortages led to increased purchases of toilet paper, which led to the shortage occurring in the first place.

Conjuring Up Exam Anxiety:

Another example of a self-fulfilling prophecy is severe *Exam Anxiety*. The expectation of failure causes anxiety and stress in the exam. This means that people tend to do worse, and the prophecy is confirmed.

Risk of accidents among seniors:

It has been shown that the more fearful seniors are of accidents such as falling downstairs and household hazards, the more likely it is that they will have more accidents because of their fear. Overly cautious behavior can invite mishaps and attract the very thing that people are most likely to avoid.

The Bank Effect:

If a credible source spreads a rumor that the bank where they have deposited their money is about to go bankrupt, people tend to withdraw their money as quickly as possible, which can lead to the bank going bankrupt due to a financial emergency that has now arisen, even if the information they had previously given was false. People follow suit because the principle applies here:
"If everyone does it that way, it must be the right thing."

The *Experimenter's Expectation Effect*:

When *Self-Fulfilling Prophecy* meets research:
The results of scientific studies can be strongly influenced by the effects of a Self-Fulfilling Prophecy. In science, this is also known as the *Experimenter's Expectation Effect*: A researcher who knows that two patients have received different medications could unconsciously treat them differently. To counteract this effect, double-blind studies are often carried out. In these studies, neither participants nor researchers know who is in the test group and who is in the control group. This prevents unconscious behavior from distorting the results of the studies.

This shows that belief can influence everyday life, so it makes sense to believe in everything you want to see in your own everyday life and specifically to block out what bothers you and is not wanted. If you express it verbally, you bring it into the world and keep it alive if you repeat it.

The senior says: *"I must be careful; I may not fall!"* And because words produce results, sooner or later he cannot help but fall. It is like balancing an egg on a spoon in your mouth. The more afraid you are of it falling, the more likely it is to happen. If you tell yourself instead that everything will be fine, you reinforce these very tendencies. You can stop worrying by telling yourself that it is a thing of the past - and do this every day for a certain period until it has become second nature, and you no longer have to repeat it.

Of course, you must clarify the facts first. But then you should let go. Otherwise, you will make a prophecy out of it that will come true sooner or later - the problem will remain or get worse. It will disappear when you stop thinking about it and you realize that problems and worries only exist in your mind, or because you had learned to repeat them constantly. If you recognize the mechanism behind it, you can say goodbye to the bad cycle.

Then you are free.

The 2nd Law

The Transformation Should Feel Familiar

Let's turn back the time for a moment:

Imagine you were your own parents and could decide which brain pathways and signposts you plant in your head. What would these look like? Be as specific as possible. If you imagine the brain as a thinking apparatus full of phrases and statements, and these phrases and statements have shaped your past - and they are currently in the process of constantly renewing your future as if in a repetition loop - then from now on, simply program and formulate these phrases yourself. As a result, you create something new that you expect and that shapes the quality and content of the phrases you repeat to yourself every day. If the formulations are like the usual phrases but are more geared to your own wishes than to those of your parents, they don't feel so foreign and therefore more familiar in a positive way. At the same time, the risk of falling back into old patterns (phrases) is reduced, because the similar goal means that there is less effort required.

I remember somebody who, at the insistence of his father, was to complete an apprenticeship as a baker and later take over the family business with several branches. He completed the training, but after that he went his own way and studied at the university the one subject that his heart was really longing for. And that was: *Nutritional Science*. First, he had to get his high school diploma to be admitted to a university. The father was angry about his son's decision and refused to support him. So, the son, who now received no state support such as student loans due to his wealthy family, had to support himself in addition to his school and academic career.

"I am living my dream life with my desired profession of ....
and I am absolutely happy with it."

He worked 80 hours a week in various catering jobs as a cook to make his living. Since his beliefs were tight enough (daily repetition, come from the heart and do not need any mental stimulation - this is how they work most strongly), he had to struggle with doubts from time to time, which were weak remnants of the old memory paths, but were still there.

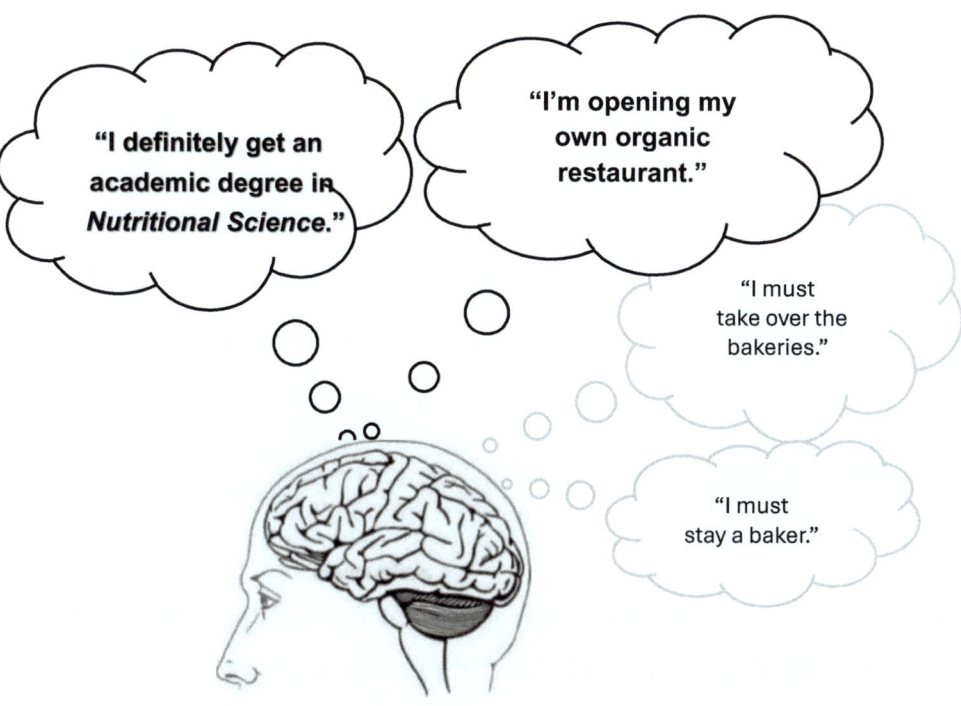

Graphic 1:

Overlaying old engrams with new, constantly repeated beliefs

Overall, the new paths are stable enough to carry him through the hard years and lead him to his goal, his dream job and his dream life. By repeating new beliefs that have become strong, old beliefs that have become superfluous or are no longer valid can be weakened.

Reality and actuality:

The Marburg brain researcher and biologist Gerhard Roth distinguishes between two different ways to look at reality:

1. consciousness-independent transphenomenal world

and

2. *phenomenal world* that is a construction of the real brain

He says: "*In reality, reality is produced by the real brain. It is therefore part of reality, namely the part in which we exist.*"

The outside is thus assigned to the outside world by internal cognitive criteria and only exists within reality:

"*I see true, not real objects.*"

But reality is not a construct of the ego, because the ego itself is only a construct of the real brain.

Roth also claims that our self was thus "... *fiction, a dream of a brain, of which we, the fiction, the dream, cannot know anything*".

In order to determine whether our perceptions reflect a real world, we would have to be able to compare our perception of the world with the real world (to be able to perceive the perception itself), but this is again only possible via our own cognitive apparatus; therefore, an individual can never know whether he or she can perceive reality or not.

One of the best-known representatives of *Radical Constructivism*, the German philosopher Ernst von Glasersfeld, said: "*...for no one will ever be able to compare the perception of an object with the postulated object itself that is supposed to have caused the perception.*"

Those theses have been refuted by the Munich philosopher Thomas Lenzen, among others, who points out that we are all capable of recognizing an objective reality and sometimes applying a subjective view to it. So, I can enter a bakery and stand next to other customers. Everyone wants to buy bread, but my idea of the cleanliness of a shop, the selection of goods and the friendliness of the salesperson can differ from the subjective assessment of other customers.

Nevertheless, we stand in the same bakery and perceive it objectively and realistically. Recognizing the subtle difference is important because it determines whether everyone lives in their own world, and there would then be more than eight billion of them, corresponding to the number of people on this planet. Or do we live in a shared world, recognize this, but still perceive the things that surround us from a personal point of view, knowing that they are part of a larger whole, but subject to our personal evaluation.

The reasons why we always attract the same people,
situations and problems lie in the arrangement
of the imprinted paths in the brain.

You cannot be different, see and experience anything different, until you have changed your personal paths - it is about literally taking "other paths". But then the new, the desired, comes almost by itself, because we are all in

- *constant interaction* with the environment and

- *constant reflection* of our inner self takes place in the outer world

We evaluate the things that happen to us, the reflection of our inner self, differently than others. A domestic, parental role model comes into play here. Mixed with our own ideas, opinions and preferences, this creates a combination of familiar (parental) and foreign (external) impressions that we try to reconcile.

The foreign can feel so much better than what we already know, but if it is too strange, we often forego a change that represents too much unknown territory. Our decisions are often still shaped by the influences of early childhood upbringing. We must overcome the fear of changing what we were told as children and stay open to the new, if we want to be and live different from what others have imprinted into our brains with reference to their ideals of how the world should be and of how and what we should become.

Neuroarchitecture

How To Reconstruct the Self

Everyone believes that they are endowed with a very personal story based on their own convictions and opinions. In fact, what we call our own story is a collection of attitudes and beliefs that are based partly on genetics, but also on the lifestyle and worldview of other people. We are shaped in the image of our former caregivers, according to the wishes of others who thought they knew how we should and must be so that they would like it best.

But how can you achieve the life that you most want for yourself? How can you live in a way that feels right and is not the life of others, that is, a life filled with values, ideals and content that have come about, at least in large part, through your own decisions and convictions?

If you believe that you are your own story, it is because you cannot distinguish between the mental content that is instilled in you and that which you have developed yourself. I am not my "story" either, but the person I have made of myself in the areas I was not happy with, because becoming completely new is difficult. You cannot block out everything you have ever learned, seen or experienced, and you don't have to; making changes where desired is enough.

You Are Not Your Story

Whenever you talk about your own story or write about it, it is important to know that this is only an excerpt, not actually your story, but just "a" story. I experienced it and survived it and do not identify with it any longer, because then I would be making the problems of other people I was/am related to my own. But I am me and someone else must come to terms with being the way they are or, if necessary, learn and adopt new attitudes. The world sees me the way I see myself. My self-image flows outwards, it shows itself in many ways: self-respect is expressed through my clothing, my appearance, a well-groomed exterior. A person with low self-esteem, on the other hand, tends to neglect their appearance.

Unkempt people often have low self-esteem, otherwise they would take better care of themselves, pay more attention to themselves and value themselves more. It is not just external appearances that are important, the inner attitude also flows through charisma, negative vibrations and a negative attitude towards others, they literally sense whether someone is in a good or bad mood, likes or dislikes themselves and others, and accepts or rejects the world as such. At first it is not so easy to change, even if everyone believes: "*My head belongs to me, I can think what I want!*" But what is one's own here is basically a self, an identity that was largely created on the drawing board by parents and those around them.

If a child is introduced to a particular religious group at an early age, with the option of possibly changing their mind later, the probability is high that they will develop a sense of belonging to the parental choice, even if it was not their own decision. This can arise 1. from a good relationship with the closest people (parents, teachers, etc.) and 2. become part of their own identity due to habits and fixed rituals (going to church on Sundays, attending parish activities, receiving the sacraments, communion, etc.).

We often take our parents as an example, adopting their views and attitudes about people, situations, politics, world events, and even their professional ambitions, which we often adopt 1:1 if they suit us. But when we identify with our parents or others, we become very similar to them and adopting their interests and goals is no longer so far-fetched for us. Then we are not just followers but become reflections of our role models.

Your mind, your way of thinking, which you believed belonged to you, is largely a copy of other people's mind and thinking, so that the number of convictions that have grown out of your own dung only make up a fraction of your mental state of being.

This can be an excellent truth for you under certain circumstances if you had supportive, loving parents with a decent character who guided and instructed you and at the same time gave you sufficient freedom of choice. Especially when it comes to essential areas of life such as relationships and starting a family, career orientation and aspirations, choice of place of residence, political opinion, but also when it comes to the development of characteristics such as thrift, friendliness, taking on responsibility and reliability, to name just a few.

Detachment from Other and Development of Own Ideals

At the end of the day, you will only find out which of these come from you when you develop your own new ideas that are different from what you have heard at some point in your immediate or wider environment. However, even here, parental or other influences can still be recognized.

For example, you grew up in an environment of highly politically active and successful people and were more than impressed by their activities, especially because of the positive relationship with them. So doing the same as them and receiving recognition for it felt like a recurring reward for you. The likelihood of becoming politically active yourself is at least increased, especially since we need our environment to form our own identity, especially at a young age. However, there is also the possibility that exactly the opposite will happen. The people around you are not very successful in what they do and so you will probably not follow in their footsteps based on the negative example and do the opposite of what you have seen and experienced here.

Someone who had addicted parents and watched their lives go down the drain is unlikely to choose to follow them. Paradoxically, however, they might, if they had a high level of respect for their parents and did not doubt anything they did or how they lived, i.e. blind obedience, even at the risk of drowning in it themselves. If they do what their role models did, they can at least be "close" to them in some way, even if it is at their own disadvantage.

I once knew a young man whose mother was an alcoholic and died too soon. For nostalgic reasons, so to speak, he also became an alcoholic; the *inner memory path* created a feeling of intimate closeness to his mother whenever he got hopelessly drunk. The logical mind already knows that this is not a good thing, but in such moments, it cannot prevail against the strong imprinting due to the imitation effect. At the same time, it is possible that exactly the opposite occurs, i.e. one develops a strong aversion to alcohol and in extreme cases cannot even drink a glass of wine at a party without a strangely unpleasant feeling (of guilt) setting in.

In both cases, your head and your thoughts do not belong to you; both behaviors, even if they are opposite, are in some way connected to early instructions from other people. The imprinting of the neural pathways therefore causes your decision whether you will one day go to the nearest university or the nearest station bar.

Description of Neural Pathways

Fortunately, it is possible to change these neural pathways. Learning new things in the desired direction causes serious changes in the external circumstances of life. However, many people wait in vain for changes that are initiated by other people from the outside, and this is not even a fallacy, because the earlier memory paths were ultimately shaped by people from the outside. It is logical that you now wait for the outside world (like parents, teachers, foreigners etc.) to bring something new into your life and continue to shape you.

Waiting for a change that others should bring you is then all too understandable, but can lead to misfortune, because not everyone has your best interests at heart. Today, only you are responsible for a change. As a child, you were shaped from the outside, i.e. "raised", and today you wait for others to offer you experience, learning processes and the expansion of your thinking. This is also pure habit and another "path" that you live every day if you believe that your hands are tied and that fate, a person or luck are responsible for the change in your life. In fact, new pathways that you integrate are responsible, because if you do this yourself, you retain control at the same time. Otherwise, you would be putting the scepter of your life in the hands of others, who could then influence your neural pathways as they wished. Some call it blind trust or devotion, but in fact it is negligent towards yourself. Even today, we are already imprinted with enough traces of others based on the experiences we have and have had with people. This can be positive for us, but just as well negative with reference to good and bad experiences.

Who and What I Am is Determined by My Environment

What bothers me on the outside is part of my own shadow that I do not want to see inside of myself. In contact with others, I get the opportunity to recognize these parts and to fix them in me. Through *Selective Perception* I only see on the outside what suits me and belongs to me, everything else is blocked out by the brain to be on the safe side due to the risk of being overwhelmed by all the impressions that exist.

Everything that is not relevant is not shown to me by my brain, although everything still exists. However, if I start to focus my inner self on other impressions, I suddenly see a new world - things, people, places that I now concentrate on.

Once I was sitting on a summer terrace with a friend and we were drinking coffee together. He told me almost casually that he wanted to go to a men's clothing store called "Stoffgarten" later that afternoon to buy a new pair of jeans. He had just finished the sentence when a white van from the company just mentioned with the inscription "Stoffgarten" drove past us. We looked at each other in surprise and were amazed at this "coincidence".

What concerns me is what I encounter on the outside. I cannot see anything that is not relevant to me, or only see it peripherally, otherwise I would see everything that exists and would be completely overwhelmed in an instant. However, I can set the filter myself and determine in advance what exactly I should encounter. If I want to study law, I must deal with everything that is related to it - and the outside world has no choice but to show me the right impressions, or my brain filters out what is right for me. Everything is there, the inner filter decides what I encounter.

The filter is already preset due to upbringing and socialization, so that my selective eye shows me everything that fits my origins and my family, especially all the impressions that give me a picture of life that my parents had chosen for me because they raised me and shaped me according to their ideas.

If I don't agree, I reset the filter using the exact (literally formulated) phrases and repeating the opposite of them, just as my inner self was shaped in this way back then - through words.

The Universe Is the Authority in Your Head

A friend once told me that she had seen an exciting film with the American actor Andy Garcia. She thought this actor was so great that she wished to meet "someone like him or similar" in person. He was her absolute dream man. The following Saturday morning she went to the nearby indoor pool to swim a few laps. Afterwards she was hungry and felt like having a portion of French fries and decided to take something to eat from the snack bar at the swimming pool before she went home. There she was served by an assistant whose sight almost made her faint with shock. He was a perfect optical copy of Andy Garcia. With this imprint, the brain had presented her with exactly the right result. Success or failure in life, life paths, opportunities and options are directly related to the paths of one's own brain.

When one speaks of a universe in this context, one means something indefinable up there that makes wishes come true. In sober terms, this is the authority up there in one's own head (brain) that leads us in the direction that we are internally set on. And then everything is possible, because everything is there, even to meet a man like Andy Garcia. If her repeated thought, which thus became a memory trace, had been different, such as: "I want to meet this Andy Garcia very clearly and specifically, marry him and be happy with him forever", why should that not have been possible? A *chain of causalities* creates connections, things, events and results that lead people in the direction they most desire deep down. Some people also thought that a man like Brad Pitt, for example, after marrying a woman like Angelina Jolie, having a whole series of children in his family, living a rich and famous life, would never be available again, because his life seemed so perfect, with everything in it that one could only dream of. But then one day he was single again and "available". Never say never.

The brain has neuroplasticity for this, i.e. its ability to change, to recreate, to form networks, to adapt to circumstances and, for example, to repair oneself after a stroke, to heal after trauma, to overcome fears and compulsions and to be able to train and improve further through targeted training. Regardless of age, we can therefore always change our behavior, learn new things and use our full potential. Various exercises strengthen the brain and thus vitality, similar to when we train the body in the gym:

Neuroplastic Exercises Change the Brain

- For example, using the cell phone with the other hand is a challenge for the brain because it must leave familiar paths
- Walking backwards: trains coordination skills
- Standing on one leg: promotes the sense of balance and strains the corresponding muscle groups.
- Solving math problems, crossword puzzles, learning a language or working on a puzzle, computer games and generally learning new skills keep the brain fit for new challenges
- The calm of meditation helps to process stress, switches off negative thoughts and inner restlessness and thus helps to heal mental imbalances
- Accordingly, progressive muscle relaxation is also useful for achieving a better body feeling and relaxation
- A good and healthy diet, drinking enough water and ensuring restful sleep and regular exercise in the fresh air improve mental fitness and are the first steps towards a healthier life that also includes mental health and the ability to cope with demands

You can also control how much negativity you allow into your own life. You don't have to watch all the news on TV all the time to stay up to date. You don't always have to be available. It is important to protect yourself, to nourish yourself, to look after yourself and to take your own needs seriously. Change is possible when you make decisions that lead in a new direction. With a strengthened body and an intact mind, you are far more courageous to tackle new things than when you feel small and weak. Strong defenses are necessary so that you can remain stable in the phases of change and reach your goal, even if there are obstacles in the way here and there.

Causal Chain - One Thing Leads to Another

Even thinking slightly differently leads to a "changed causal chain": Why does negative attract more negative and positive attract more positive? A causal chain is the term for several causes that follow one another in time and that, when combined, produce a certain effect. In *Attribution Theory*, simple cause-effect relationships are generally examined. In real life, however, causes are often connected in a complex way when they produce an effect. This is especially true in the case of causes that follow one another in time and that, when combined, produce an effect that occurs later. When two causal causes follow one another, the question arises as to which cause is considered more important. An everyday example is a young person who commits shoplifting. His behavior can be explained by the fact that his father left the family early. Another explanation is that his mother became an alcoholic at a later point in time. So, whenever you start something new, you set a process in motion that attracts similar things and adds them to the actual process via a body-environment connection. You can become interested in a particular topic, and as a result you will keep encountering new impressions that are somehow related to what you are thinking about. It is important that you do not throw in the towel and give up at the classic problem point that occurs with every change. The natural fears or the typical discomforts that arise as soon as you deal with something new must not become an obstacle that prevents people from taking the path they want.

The following model uses a professional example to show how one step on the path of change leads to the next step, how old thought patterns can be changed, but then can be hindered by negative emotions, and how a relaxed attitude can still allow you to achieve your goals confidently and calmly. As a result, you can see new effects that show a decisive change in life.

The 5E – Model of Life Change

Diametrical opposite

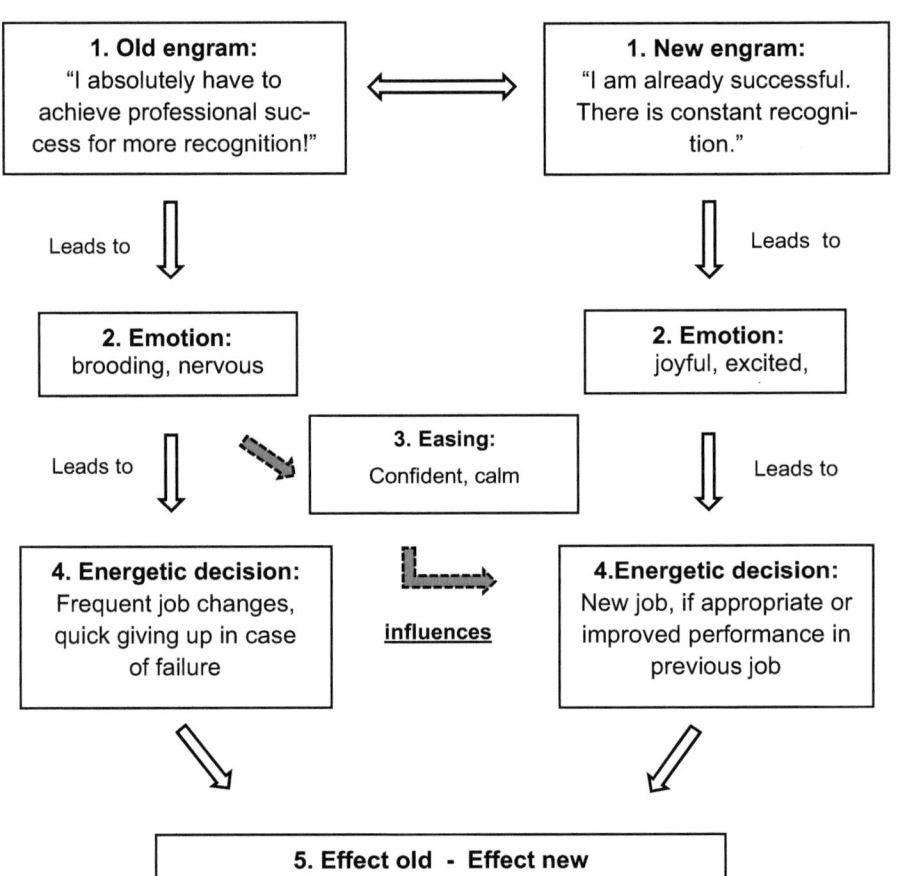

| 1. Old engram: "I absolutely have to achieve professional success for more recognition!" | ⟺ | 1. New engram: "I am already successful. There is constant recognition." |

Leads to ⟱

2. Emotion: brooding, nervous

Leads to ⟱ → **3. Easing:** Confident, calm

4. Energetic decision: Frequent job changes, quick giving up in case of failure

⌐---→ influences

Leads to ⟱

2. Emotion: joyful, excited,

Leads to ⟱

4. Energetic decision: New job, if appropriate or improved performance in previous job

5. Effect old - Effect new
Insecure Employment – Clear Professional

The Austrian psychologist Werner Stangl states that *engram* is now a general term for the coding and storage of the experience acquired over the course of a lifetime in the neurons of the brain. The sum of a person's stored engrams is considered the biological substrate of human memory and is the basis of specific human uniqueness. An engram refers to all electrochemical processes (short-term memory) or biochemical changes (long-term memory) in the central nervous system that underlies a memory content (the memory of a situation). The ability to form a memory is an essential property that enables learning and the accumulation of knowledge.

Engrams are like "brands" that make it so difficult to get rid of a stressful educational model. Negative engrams can be overlaid by positive engrams. The earlier a memory trace was created, the more strongly it works in the person, and it is almost impossible to erase it.

When change occurs, one feels restlessness; if this is calmed down through relaxation, a new, future effect can be perceived.

The Power of "Engrams"

Phrases that Create Identity

Engrams are brain imprints - "instilled commands in the head" that are active every day until you stop them, change them and transform them into new habits through regular repetition.

There is a miracle in our brain, a universe of its own. Even the smallest learning process, whether it is the first word, the first finger pointing or the complex mathematical formula - what we have memorized through constant repetition, may stay with us for a lifetime - provided we repeat it, at least from time to time, and thus keep it "fresh". What we do not repeat, in word and deed, is classified by the brain as "not useful" and fades over time.

These memory traces, which are firmly anchored in the brain through repetition, serve as orientation for people, as signposts and direction markers for all big and small decisions.

For example, if young people do not wear "cool" clothes at school, they may be excluded. The feeling of rejection that has already been experienced is perceived as extremely unpleasant and the resulting memory trace ("engram") can be reinforced by further similar experiences. The deepest-seated engrams are also the biggest driving forces of our everyday lives. They guide and lead us, tell us what and how we should do something. They structure our day routinely and drive the car on the way home like an internal navigation device. In addition, they navigate all movements and the directions we go in. They have the power in a universe that we call our life.

These engrams are permeated with emotions, positive or negative, because we are most likely to learn the things that we like to do or the things that cause us pain. The hand on the hot stove, the forgotten key in the apartment, the failed exam. Or the necessary application that led to the dream job, the lottery win, challenges that were overcome well. Everything is imprinted on us due to an accompanying feeling that we perceive as good or bad. The decisive factor is the power of the feeling behind the impression, which turns it into a formative experience. What we no longer need and no longer feel goes into a mental "graveyard of engrams". Sometimes we visit the graves inside, perhaps shed an imaginary tear, feel a residual emotion, remember briefly and then turn to the engrams that are currently being used and felt, because they determine the life of everyone today. The good ones give me all the good around me, the negative ones the bad. If I want to change things in my environment, I must initiate new learning processes, because this is the only key to change.

Practicing desired processes, which form engrams in the brain through learning units, follows a pattern that I call the 5E formula.

1. **Engram –**

   imprinting a new path

2. **Emotion –**

   developing a suitable feeling

3. **Easing –**

   opening up with trust

4. **Energetic Decision –**

   courage to say yes and act

5. **Effect –**

   allowing the effect to show

Step 1 - Change Engram:

Form new phrases that become new memory paths by training them every morning, i.e. memorizing them until they no longer feel strange but familiar. Through direct and indirect interaction with the environment, new people, situations and events will emerge, just as your life up to now was formed from the old phrases or memory paths and resulted in the details. When the inner words change, this has a direct influence on behavior, appearance and dealing with others, but also an indirect influence on events, occurrences and reactions of life itself, which is diametrically opposed to us. Not only do the people around us respond to the person, life itself also responds to how we deal with ourselves and communicate.

Step 2 - Promote Emotion:

Of course, we all only want the people, things and moments that we like from the bottom of our hearts. Therefore, fill your phrases with the appropriate emotion, imagine the fulfillment of the new and enjoy how completion feels. Appropriate adjectives encourage the formation of emotions because they give the words the necessary passion. Phrases formulated with passion can activate feelings. Just as a nice compliment can generate joy, formulating statements with positive terms is an accelerator for feelings that can create a good aura and inner connections.

Step 3 - Make A Decision:

If you align your new decisions with the changed engrams, you will no longer make decisions based on old beliefs, otherwise the external results will remain the same and nothing would change. New thinking creates new decisions. New decisions are the basis for new experiences. A yes to a certain side simultaneously includes a no to the opposite side. If things are to change, decisions are part of it, even if it is difficult to let go of things you love or hate, because you have become used to everything that happens to you every day, including the bad things. You can only live better if you overwrite the old decisions and dare to really take the new direction.

Step 4 - Create Easing:

It is not always easy for people to create new mental paths, because the rational mind cannot (or does not want to) imagine changing life and everyday scenarios or because fear gets in the way (see the chapter on *Crocodile Bridge*). Then it is time to let go and put the plan aside for the time being. This automatically leads to relaxation and from here you can try again. The tension often comes because the brain initially has difficulty with change. If you give up the plan, the inner calm has a relieving effect and takes away the frightening importance of things.

For example, if you have an unfulfilled desire to have children, it makes sense to give up trying, at least for the time being. Internal blockages that were caused by rigidly holding on, among other things, dissolve and change becomes possible.

Example - Desire for a partner:

If the search for a new relationship is too dogged, this basically shows that you have doubts about whether you will achieve personal happiness. The less you believe in success, the harder you try, whereas calmness is often a sign of confidence in achieving your goal. If I know that success will come, no matter what it is, I don't have to try so hard. Fears often lead people to give more than is necessary. These doubts and fears may then show up externally as blockages and in the form of obstacles, which is why it may be important to give up the goal at first so that a relaxed inner attitude can develop. From this, a new attempt to imprint suitable and desired engrams can be initiated, but this time without pressure or fear, as the idea of achieving a goal is handled much more calmly.

Step 5 - Perceive Effects:

The effects show how things are going inside you, whether you have managed to establish the memory pathways through constant repetition and can now recognize the results and changes within your own world.

If no desired results are seen and the old continues to repeat itself, you can tell that the previous engrams are still having a strong effect on you and that new phrases still need to be practiced so that doubts no longer have any room.

The 3rd Law

The Transformation Should Be Effective and Permanent

Everything changes when you plan for new phrases/mantras/brain inscriptions. Since the environment is our mirror and there is a strong inner connection between people and their external social structure, the new positive phrases are like "game changers" that push people into improved life situations.

Everyone wants these processes to simply take place, especially in times when new things are coming up. But because it hasn't always worked that way, many people are reluctant to any kind of change. New things are frightening. But there is a remedy. If you set the alarm clock and save improved phrases at the same time, your feeling, charisma and personal orientation for the entire day will be different.

In the morning after waking up, we are most receptive to external influences, as well as to the thoughts that we are most preoccupied with. During the night, the brain has processed events from the previous day, and the most intense events had to be "digested". With the right words, you motivate yourself and create the willingness to open yourself to everything that was simply waiting for the clear starting signal.

Instead of this, better phrases could be:

"Abundance! There is enough of everything.
More and more money is coming from a variety of sources
right in my direction."

"My financial source keeps bubbling and bubbling
and will never end."

When we wake up, we find ourselves in a state of relaxation, unless more persistent problems that still need to be solved gnawing at our souls. Then they return to you as soon as you wake up. These can be existential fears that exert pressure in the stomach area early in the morning and make their concerns clearly and distinctly visible all the way up to our consciousness. The thoughts that then prevail are usually based on familiar phrases that we often learned in childhood. Today, because they are branded into our brain structures, they keep coming back to our consciousness in a stereotypical way that suits the current situation.

"Everything is just getting worse and worse. I have no chance, and my plans aren't going to come to fruition anyway. I'm always bankrupt/I can't achieve anything."

These are typical, externally instilled inefficient phrases that are activated at any time as soon as a suitable topic arises (here: existential fear). However, if you put yourself in a better mood, increase your inner energies (e.g. with the help of positive adjectives), it is like saying "yes" to what you want to experience. Through external reflection, what is already there but is still invisible to the person who feels discordant is then made visible. In other words, as soon as you

- focus on what you want to see in your own life and
- don't focus on what you fear,

the curtain opens by itself, and you see things that have always been there anyway, just you looked in the other way.

The Secret Life of Adjectives

You can formulate a phrase neutrally if it is about a simple matter. Let's take the example of someone who wants to increase the salary from 3,5k to 7k a month. There is a certain probability that a higher income will not be achieved if previous conditioning continues to lead to doubts about the realization of the goal.

Perhaps if you come from a poorer home or have been taught that money, success and reputation are somehow negatively associated you struggle with even these achievements. However, if you attach an emotion to the phrase, it will find its way through the *invisible connection with the outside world* and trigger events, situations and opportunities that give shape to emotionalized thoughts and ultimately make them come true.

Then the simple phrase of wanting more at some point becomes a highly motivated one:

**"I am absolutely thrilled
to be earning 7,000,00 a month now!"**

Enthusiasm, joy, the feeling of happiness, any positive assessment transforms a neutral phrase into one with a *magnetic effect* that draws out of life and the world exactly what the phrase demands in terms of content.

A series of positive adjectives that you can use to describe your new phrases:

breathtaking, attractive, brilliant, inspiring, grateful, unique, first-class, excellent, fantastic, joyful, delighted, brilliant, happy, grandiose, great, splendid, intense, precious, passionate, luxurious, magical, fairytale-like, thrilling, gripping, perfect, splendid, rich, beautiful, sensational, spectacular, exciting, strong, dream-like, overwhelming, wonderful, super, great.

The phrase therefore consists of a factual and an emotional part. The factual part contains what it is about, and the part emotionalized by the adjective turns the entire sentence into a magnet that connects with the outside world and, due to the constructivist perception, attracts exactly the content mentioned. The content is the *message* that you send out and the adjective is the *messenger* that picks up what has been formulated from the outside and delivers it to the sender. That is why it is so important to formulate your content precisely, to state in detail what the goal should look like and what you specifically have in mind.

"I want to develop further my education."

…should become:

"I am excited that I am now graduating as a programmer!"

– is the key to realization, because we perceive exactly what we concretize.

Thought + Feeling= Result

If you were to describe your current situation in just one sentence, you would get something like:

"I am alone and feel lonely" or *"I hate that I don't earn enough and my bills are too high"* or *"I am not happy with my job, I am waiting for/trying to get better offers"* or *"The work week is so stressful and tiring, I never have time for myself"* or *"It makes me sad that no one ever calls me."*

It is true that the descriptions apply exactly to the current situations and events and reflect them, but things cannot get better if you constantly think about what is wrong in your own life instead of developing a positive vision for the future and formulating it in your own words.

The Rule is: **Thought - Feeling = Result.**

Because thoughts trigger feelings and these are in constant social interaction with the environment, this creates a visible result on the outside. You can therefore bring about results with the help of feelings if you stop "judging" your own situation and instead use formulations that, equipped with positive adjectives, represent the expected new and better in the current state.

"I am happy that I still have enough time for myself, my hobbies and interests alongside my work."

"I think it is very nice that people keep contacting me and asking about me."

"I am happy that I am earning more and more and that it keeps rising up to... € (state a specific amount)."

With thoughts you formulate what you want, with feelings you establish the connection to the outside, which as a kind of source provides the desired goods. This connection is always created through feelings, because they are the driving force and the magnet for the realization or failure of one's own plans, wishes and goals. Positive plans come from thoughts, positive adjectives create the feeling, the feeling influences the interaction with what I can perceive in my environment through the constructivist approach. The feeling directs the inner compass to everything that should become visible in one's own life. Equipping every plan, every goal in the now with suitable adjectives has a similar effect on the body as the method of *Progressive Muscle Relaxation* developed in the 1920s by the American doctor Edmund Jacobsen. Here, too, you say positive words to yourself and focus on physical areas that you want to relax. The word, the phrase triggers a positive feeling in the body if you focus on it precisely. Pleasant words create an inner feeling of well-being, allow muscles to relax and good feelings to arise - and this feeling is the key to the outside world.

If I say to myself in the morning: *"Today is a wonderful day with many beautiful events and lovely encounters."* - then the adjectives in the sentence ensure that this mental image is realized, because an adjective is able to trigger a feeling. Three adjectives triple the feeling and show the environment the reflection of these own emotional messages. The feeling creates the inner opening for what one could not recognize before but was nevertheless there. If you now become specific and name a desired current state with positive adjectives, then the outside cannot help but reflect exactly this, because the inner world is spiritual and the outer world is material, i.e. this effect is simply the logical consequence of mirror reflection.

Reflecting the experienced feeling is the appropriate echo that embodies the copy of the feeling presented on a material level. If you say: "*I am very pleased with the excellent relationship with my colleagues!*" - the appropriate result will appear when the adjectives trigger the corresponding feeling, i.e. you put aside doubts and rejection. If you say the opposite, such as: "*I don't like all these disgusting people around me, their ugly manner run me down!*" - you shouldn't be surprised if you get what you had already emotionally "predicted" beforehand. So, it makes little sense to try to work on the outside world. You make the prediction internally and your own constructivist worldview does the rest, showing and revealing exactly the impressions that were already there but only became apparent through your own inner opening.

The "Crocodile Bridge"

No Power to Fear

The biggest problem and obstacle to change is that, on the one hand, we want to leave familiar paths, but on the other hand, our brain also finds security and peace in what we have "always done" and is firmly embedded in our everyday lives.

When we strive for something new, a feeling of unease regularly arises after a short time, and we throw all our plans out the window and go back to what we know, even if it is not good for us. We should persevere, and always exactly when something like a perceived "crocodile bridge" appears. We must cross it if we really want life to get better. Its appearance is part of the process of changing our lives and is completely normal.

When desired changes are made, one often must cross an imaginary bridge from current location A to desired location B, where threats appear that seem like *dangerous crocodiles* just waiting to attack. These are one's own fears and doubts that always make themselves known when a person leaves familiar paths. The further you progress on the bridge (i.e., practice new habits through repetition), the fewer the *crocodiles* there are and the less danger there is. When you reach point B, they have completely disappeared. You have shown life that you cannot be intimidated.

The brain loves its routine: for example, two cups of mild roasted coffee in the morning with some oat milk, a slice of wholemeal bread with cottage cheese and cocktail tomatoes, chives and the daily dose of magnesium and vitamin C and you are ready to start the new day. The breakfast habits listed can be imagined as engrams imprinted in the memory, i.e. inner mental paths that guide people blindly through their everyday lives as soon as they wake up. By using processes and routines that have become established through repetition, the brain saves energy for other, new activities. These, in turn, feel strange at first until they are established inside. If the brain then classifies them as useful and meaningful and repeats them with a certain frequency, the storage process takes place again, inner rejections disappear, and they are assigned to existing routines as further familiar units.

This transition phase between

A.) the desire to let something new into your life and
B.) the point at which it has become ingrained as a memory path

can be imagined as a suspension bridge in the jungle. You *must* cross it if you really want to experience something new or change.

Crocodiles swim down there that scare you, they want you to go back to the beginning of the bridge, to stay where you were, in your old life, as it was, and for nothing to change. The crocodiles are your own worries, grown out of prohibitions and experiences. A precautionary measure, because you don't know how the new thing will develop. But if you want to change, you have to expect that the bridge will open first. This is one of the reasons why so many stay in bad jobs and unhappy relationships, because when they take a step forward towards change, they are putting their first foot on the bridge, and the feeling that then occurs can be more unpleasant than the actual life situation itself.

The "fear memory", the hippocampus, is the *GPS* in the brain, responsible for orientation and navigation in space, filters information from the higher areas of the cerebral cortex and forms appropriate signals from the selection. The "bouncers" stand at the entrance to the hippocampus circuit and are granule cells (a type of neuron). An experience of fear, for example, activates these cells so that they send information to engrams and thus ensure stable memories (from a biological point of view through a protein with an epigenetic factor). Cells store fear in engrams and fear experiences thus become established memory pathways. If you inactivate these neurons, you change your own "fear memory".

Why is it so difficult to change a behavior that has already become ingrained? Before birth and in the first years of life, the brain is still very plastic – it is changeable. At the end of puberty at the latest, the plasticity of the brain decreases significantly. The brain thinks more and more often:

"Enough testing!
These changes are too much work for me now."

The brain rewards us for the building of habits by repetition with its own opioids. We become dependent on them. Over the course of life, the effort to change a habit increases steadily. But where are habits in the brain?

When we learn something for the very first time, it is controlled by our cerebral cortex. After repeating it frequently or even several times, this behavior becomes routine. The resulting speaking information slips into our basal ganglia deep inside the brain. There it is stored as fixed processes that can no longer be erased. Overriding an old habit with a new one is therefore one of the most difficult things there is.

What Is the Best Way to Motivate Myself?

Only a few factors can fundamentally change our behavior. In addition to repetition, it requires suffering because of negative circumstances in life or the prospect of reward that want us to make a change. It is particularly helpful if the behavior is linked to a person to whom we are strongly attached. The final kick for the willingness to change usually comes from outside. The more you look forward to the new and are open to it, the less you will perceive the transition from old to new as threatening; and then the *crocodiles* may not even appear. Your positive vision of a better future supported by positive affirmations and phrases enriched by great adjectives, will constantly reduce your inner rejections and take you to places where you really want to live, work and be.

From Poor Brain to Money Brain

A woman once used a simple trick to transform her fear brain into a trust brain, and she did it with just one phrase that she said to herself once a day. She had just lost her job because she was not willing to work at another of her employer's locations in moldy and therefore unhealthy rooms. She was dismissed without further ado, as she was still in her probationary period. A few applications that she sent out were subsequently unsuccessful. But now she was not entitled to unemployment benefits, so she was very worried about what would happen next.

Every morning, she woke up at around 5 a.m. with the unpleasant feeling of inner panic, not knowing what the new day would bring and whether she would still be able to afford to buy food in a month. But she knew that hope and despair are closely related and that a large part of the fears we carry around with us come from old experiences and feelings from childhood - and therefore often no longer have any reality today. It is normal to worry in uncertain times and to be scared about changes. Something is getting out of hand and when there is no solution in sight, you feel uncomfortable (the brain loves routine and the familiar).

That is why she relied more on the principle of hope than on the suffering of brooding and created a morning phrase that she now recited to herself like a mantra every day when she woke up. Since she had saved the phrase in her cell phone and let it wake her up frequently, she had it in front of her as soon as the phone rang in the mornings, and she looked at it to turn off the alarm.

"There is always only abundance,
I live in prosperity -
everything is always available in sufficient quantities!"

Over time, she developed an abundance consciousness, because her brain learned a new routine that gave her confidence that she no longer had to worry.

But every now and then, the old fears and doubts kicked in again: *"Why shouldn't I worry? My situation hasn't changed. When will it get better? What will happen next, I don't know what's coming!"*

But she realized that this was just the old fear again, which, out of a familiar routine, had to make itself known again from time to time. But she stuck to her sentence and repeated it stereotypically, not knowing what was coming, and she stayed on the ball professionally and kept her eyes open. Little by little, new opportunities and even opportunities for self-employment arose and soon things were going so well for her that she had an income like never before. Whenever the fear brain came up with the old fears, she calmed down with the phrase:

"Abundance –
there is enough of everything, more than enough!"

And she also convinced herself that it was not just a saying, but that it corresponded to reality.

There is more than enough money in the world, who could deny that? So, it is true to think like that, to believe in abundance, because abundance surrounds us when we look at it, instead of at the lack that is also present. The focus we choose is relevant. At the same time, the belief in abundance leads to feeling financially secure in this world, because it has more than enough of everything. Then the woman went a step further: After she had now implemented her wish to acquire independent contracts with a volume of 5,000,00 per month on her own initiative based on her skills, she thought to herself:

"What I say will happen.
Why shouldn't I just aim for 6k a month?"

But the fear of mind intervened again, worrying her and showing new doubts. *"6k ? That's too much!"* But she believed in the possibility and simply added a second phrase to her "abundance" phrase:

"I'm so happy and glad that I now earn 6k a month!"

And thanks to the positive feeling and joy that she associated with the specific amount, she was soon able to look forward to 6k monthly income. Then she thought:

"Why not 7, 8 or 9k...?!"

When we are born, we all have the same opportunities - what separates us are the circumstances into which we were born. It is the intellectual content of the brain that decides which group in society we belong to, even if we were initially born into a world that, due to its political, geographical and/or social situation, seemed to have little promise for our advancement. The way of looking at life leads people to better worldly regions that can be more advantageous for the individual or leaves the same person in old patterns, so that he or she remains very far from a transformation of circumstances.

"It's so great!
My wealth keeps increasing and increasing and increasing
and it keeps increasing and increasing and increasing!"

It is up to us to change things with the help of the right beliefs. There is enough money in this world, no one could deny that. So, you are not lying to yourself when you say:

"There is definitely enough of everything."

On the contrary - you calm yourself down if you are struggling with existential fears, you give yourself courage and at the same time you set the inner course so that you finally open yourself up to what already exists in the world, but you yourself could not imagine being able and allowed to share in large incomes due to your individual financial conditioning. Now the way is clear, new

memory paths lay the foundation for the reflection on the outside, an image of what we now are on the inside:
becoming, being and staying rich.

"I'm so excited that money is coming to me from all sorts of sources!"

In the beginning there was the word. And it became reality. It's best to determine how much you want to earn per month. It should be an amount that you can imagine. If you carry a home-made check for three million Euros in your wallet but can't imagine the amount in your own account because you set it too high and you just can't realize the image inside, the chances of even reaching that amount are slim. You achieve what you can imagine and consider "normal". That's why it's better to start small and increase slowly.

What amount would feel feasible and achievable today? Maybe 10,000? If that's too much, you should start smaller again. What you think you can do, you achieve, what you can feel inside has the potential to become reality. What I say from my heart will happen, what I don't feel will not reach me, not even in 100 years.

Sources of money exist everywhere, and donations can appear permanently. You don't have to think about where money comes from, it is already available in abundance. The task for everyone is to transform themselves into the right person, to create the appropriate financial phrases and to repeat them daily so that the external sources "learn" in which direction and to whom they should flow. Even if you think you are open to more, the actual result afterwards is the measure of your own willingness to let money, or a lot of money come into your life.

From Pain Brain to Healing Brain

Every person can decide for themselves every day whether to think in terms of pain or healing. Illness, discomfort and all other health problems initially lead to the person thinking about the issue, because the brain is always trying to regenerate, improve and heal.

That is why we often think about our problems - we want to find solutions, balance out situations, heal. And until that happens, our thoughts constantly revolve around a situation in our life that is not right, until we either find solutions or the matter is not important enough and fizzles out.

Everything revolves around mental and physical problems, the brain is under the influence of an ever-burning floodlight of negativity, which of course produces no solutions or tends to produce only negative ones. It would be better to use the skills of the healing brain.

There is a difference between an illness-mentality and a health-mentality:

"I'm not feeling well because Mr./Mrs. XY is bothering me with behavior XY. Then he/she said this and that to me, then I responded this and that, then he/she said, then I said…"

"Besides, my knee hurts again, my elbow is constantly hurting, my back hurts and I've had a migraine since this morning."

"What therapy can I do next, where can I find someone who is suitable for me to treat, what is the right recipe, behavior, the right application?"

How about:

"Fortunately, the problem has already been solved – it is a thing of the past!"

"Fortunately, I'm now feeling better and better and better every day."

When you practice autogenic training for example, you realize that internal sentences that are specifically directed at an area of the body bring warmth, relaxation and loosening to that area. Thoughts can positively influence the body and all its sensitivities.

The *Coué Method*

The French pharmacist Emile Coué (1857-1927) had experienced through advising his customers, who bought their medicines from his store, how much a positive word from him seemed to improve people's sensitivities. He said goodbye to everyone who entered his pharmacy and bought medicines there with the words:

"From now on,
you will feel better and better every day."

Much positive feedback later encouraged him to continue to work on autosuggestion. He had found that in an illness the psychological condition often overshadows the physical and thus the mental part of the illness must first be healed so that the physical aspect can follow and heal as well. Every sentence spoken would influence the body and mind via the ears. He further described that we possess within ourselves a force of inestimable power which, if we use it unconsciously, often becomes a disadvantage to us. On the contrary, if we use it consciously and wisely, it gives us control over ourselves and enables us not only to escape physical and mental suffering, but also to find a life of relative happiness, regardless of the conditions in which we find ourselves.

The Coué method states that the mind can hold onto certain ideas in the cognitive area and that with sufficient intensity a dominant idea begins to function unconsciously as a "suggestion", which in turn is biophysical, spontaneously and involuntarily.

"Every idea that has been sufficiently strongly imprinted strives to be realized and will be realized, provided that no laws of nature stand in the way."

Émile Coué (1857-1926)

The *Carpenter Effect*

This would also be the realization of an "ideodynamic principle", like the *Carpenter Effect*, named after the British natural scientist William B. Carpenter (1813-1885), also known as the *Ideomotor Effect*. This describes the phenomenon of how seeing a movement can cause others to perform this movement and think about the movement. The mere idea of a movement therefore triggers a reaction in the muscle area.

More recent studies using electrophysiological methods confirmed this psychomotor law (*ideomotor law*). So, if the "idea" embodied in Coué's formula was repeated relentlessly over a longer period, the body could follow it over time. And from the interaction between body, mind and environment, this would not only influence mental and physical health, but also an effect on the personal environment, since decisions, thoughts and actions are reflected here and can cause *feedback effects*.

This means that conscious and unconscious thinking and the resulting actions can trigger a kind of echo of the environment and reflect to the person to what extent their thinking promotes positive, neutral or negative reactions.

The *Kohnstamm Phenomenon*

In 1915, the neurologist and psychiatrist Oskar Kohnstamm (1813-1917) discovered a phenomenon in which, after a period of inner mental tension, the body reacted with muscular tension. Unconsciously, an intensive thought process can, for example, trigger twitching, as most people know in stressful situations when the eye suddenly shows uncontrollable muscle reactions. Accordingly, there is an unconscious coordination between body and mind.

The anxious brain, i.e. thinking focused on fears and worries, therefore contributes directly and indirectly to the fact that neutral situations tend to develop less favorably for those affected. Whereas a healing mindset has a positive impact on the fact that good and hopeful thinking triggers more well-being and can promote an improvement in the respective situation. Here, too, the healing sentence should not be directed at a point in the future, but the target situation should be formulated in the present.

"I'm getting better and better and better,"

has a different effect than:

"One day I'll feel better again."

Because only in the present can you achieve your goals, the future is a construct of the mind that has no reality. Likewise, the past has no reality, it only exists in our memory. In this present, we can determine for ourselves how we feel and what we want to expect.

"Read this every day
and your life will change."

Bob Proctor (1934-2022, author and lecturer)

Get The Magic Wand!

Recommendations For Education and Society

Not only can each individual benefit from the blessings of personally designed phrases, which, through constant repetition, lead life in new directions as memory paths. Parents, teachers and institutions can also motivate children, other people entrusted to them or employees to reach new heights with the gift of appreciation.

Upbringing and parents' home:

If the mother says to her child with a certain regularity (repetition):

"I find it frustrating to realize that you're not going to amount to anything!",

…then this has different consequences for the child's future than if she were to use other phrases.

"I believe in you 100% and I'll always support you!"

… can motivate new achievements and turn a child who is perhaps actually in a phase of laziness into a person who is ready to show more responsibility and more diligence. If creative, targeted design of memory pathways is started early, adolescents can be guided in successful directions, just as in the past the opposite was often achieved through incorrect linguistic elements that were internalized and then did more harm than good.

What would this world look like if, for example, post-war generations had not given their children a vision of the future of suffering, pain and grief, if they had first experienced healing from their experiences through "*phrase therapy*" and then been able to be a better father or mother. How success-oriented but also empathetic and compassionate could new generations of teachers be who developed high-quality, communication-based guidelines that motivate children, young people and adults to exploit their potential further than before? It makes a difference whether a child starts the day with a positive, indifferent or negative approach.

The young person who has gone astray and who no one believes is capable of anything could focus on his or her strengths that may not have been recognized until now and thus give life a decisive turn. Using skills means using resources for the benefit of the individual and in the service of society when these are available in a wide variety of areas.

Healing generational trauma

Old beliefs are passed down through generations. But the worries and needs of post-war generations are not identical to the problems and conflicts of generations in the 21st century. They cannot be compared. Today we are less threatened by hunger and more by digital attacks, computer viruses and cyber-attacks. The problems always depend on the time in which we live. But the human brain does not know this difference - it bases its predictions of the future on past experiences.

And when houses and bridges were destroyed and there was a shortage of bread, it sends exactly these images out to subsequent generations, who are probably not affected by this at all. But you can learn to think differently. The emotionally disturbing images will most likely not disappear, but better images and, above all, phrases can be used to counter them. We must question our traumas in terms of their real content.

"Do my thoughts have reality? Are they real?"

And then you usually realize that they have no reality, unless it is a current conflict. If not, and this is usually the case with traumas that happened a long time ago, then they only exist as a thought in your head, like an air bubble that you let burst. However, if you believe that the thought has reality, the brain usually fools the person affected into thinking that it still does, because it cannot emotionally distinguish the past moment from the present moment in memory. But we can be attentive and recognize this.

"Is it reality or is it just a thought?"

… is then the question that opens the eyes of those affected at the critical moment and brings the truth to light. And the truth can take away the burden of a trauma.

Many generations stereotypically go to a social welfare office, job center or employment agency because it is part of the family tradition to not work and to rely on financial state support. Here too, it is the wrong upbringing that has shaped people in that they adopt the behavior, attitude and morals of caregivers who send young people out into life without any chance or prospects, without knowing that there is something else besides the life they were born into.

It is above all the task of social workers to show these prospects to future generations when parents are not able to do this, because their own phrases have usually become too entrenched for them to even want to change them.

Then you can hear them saying sentences like:

**"If I were younger, I would try to live differently,
but now it's no longer worth it."**

But now again, it becomes a plan, not to be worth it to make a change, however, change would still be senseful for the generations to come, when the speaker leaves his legacy to the descendants. Transformation is not a question of age. But if you say this phrase often enough, it might hit home for the person who prophesies it.

We must understand that our memorized paths are our signposts for the future.

We don't have to do much for that; what we repeat in our minds every day comes back to us as feedback from life, even if we didn't want it to. If we are mindful and choose the words we say to others, but especially those we say to ourselves, so that they reflect what we really want in life, then why should a life that we have been given as a gift not hear us and let us suffer? There is no scientifically plausible reason for this. Life wants to survive, so it must be positive towards us. And that is the only thing that makes logical sense.

If the manager of a company says to his or her employee in the annual review:

"You need to try harder; your sales are lower than last year, I don't even know what I'm paying you for", then this has different consequences for the employee's future work as if the manager would have said something different like: *"You've done an excellent job. We're glad we have you. How can we support you and your potential even more broadly within the company?"*

In the areas of skills training and development, it has long been clear that everyone can do anything, no matter what. The construction worker can carry a heavy stone, not everyone can do that, and this gives him or her an advantage when it comes to earning money. On closer inspection, a man with reduced mental abilities can have the ability to move furniture up a narrow staircase or prepare creative meals with passion - if you tell him from the start that he can't do anything and is useless, you would be denying him the right to a self-determined and self-financed life, depriving the society that we all are of valuable resources and at the same time possibly destroying a person's self-esteem and inner satisfaction. But even in the context of an intellectually completely opposite direction, incorrect sentences that do not fit the person and character of the recipient can have fatal consequences for the individual as well as for society.

The legendary Prague writer Franz Kafka (1883-1924), for example, had no intention of taking over his parents' haberdashery business, or so it is said. He wanted to be a writer. But to do justice to his parents in some way, he studied law and earned a doctorate in law. As a newly qualified attorney, he took a job at an insurance company and, with little joy in his work, lived a life that he had not chosen himself, at least during the day. At night, he lived his true calling and wrote his world-famous, timeless texts. How much greater would the enrichment have been for him, his family and the world if his true core had not been avoided, but rather perceived correctly and allowed to exist.

Let us tell ourselves, but also all those we know, like and love, exactly what corresponds to their true potential, what suits them. Let us tell ourselves every day where we are now, where we would like to see ourselves now, and what we say will happen, if we believe.

To do this, however, you must try and practice looking at the world objectively at least now and then, i.e. looking beyond your own subjectivist view to be able to judge how someone else feels, i.e. empathize with someone else's world, even if it is not what you feel. Whenever you try to walk in someone else`s shoes, you understand and feel that is more than one world and that we all have the right to be understood in our own individual mindset.

Overcoming Relationship Trauma

We have learned to make judgements and evaluations about the relationships that shaped our past. Even in childhood, we had to deal with disappointments; the people we cared for were not always as perfect as we had expected.

For the child, mom and dad are the whole world. If it does not receive unconditional love, this world is shattered, because it learns that love must be earned, otherwise it will not come. But even if you as a child do your job, a few words of praise may follow, but here too you wait in vain for attention that goes beyond a brief and usually superficial interest. Because - if they do not love you unconditionally, they also do not love you when the conditions are met as they cannot love at all, whatever you bring to the table. The pretense of fulfilling the conditions is usually just an excuse for the inability to love and it is not immediately apparent, and so the unloving father or mother is not directly to blame.

If the child does not perform, be it school grades, good behavior, manners, helpfulness towards others, everything that narcissistic parents can benefit from, then they are labelled as not good enough and the lack of love is supposedly their own fault. With this first experience of love, the child grows up and goes out into the world. The relationships that follow are often a reflection of the kind of love that was already experienced in the parental home. This gives rise to beliefs:

"I am not good enough, I can never please others."

"I am not lovable, no matter what I do,
nobody takes me seriously."

This creates another bad cycle, a self-fulfilling prophecy. Now the former children do not speak well of themselves as they became adults, but this is what they should do to turn the tide. Otherwise, the damaged parental love experienced is renewed again and again, often until the end of one's life.

So, when it comes to relationships, you don't have to wait for the right partner, you just have to say the right things to each other. And you should have the courage to cross the *Crocodile Bridge* again because it always appears, not only when there is a concrete danger, but also when the brain makes a prediction about the future based on previous experiences.

If you have been disappointed, you believe that former events might happen to you again and again. The protective mechanism is activated as soon as a similar, familiar situation arises, and you either go for a confrontation *("fight")* or you seek to escape *("flight")*.

One method of creating a fresh start in deadlocked relationships is for partners who no longer trust each other to meet on a bridge on a specific day and at a specific time. If both go to the agreed meeting, it means that from now on they are starting from scratch in their relationship and forgiving each other for everything that led to the loss of trust, faith and loyalty. It is not allowed to meet on the bridge and then bring up old accusations again. If they appear there, everything will be forgiven and forgotten - and everything is new and starts from scratch.

It makes a difference in your life, if you walk into the day with the attitude of:

"I know my next relationship will be great, the best and most beautiful relationship I've ever had."

… because then life can't help but present in the feedback what you honestly consider to be your mantra through constant repetition, and this becomes a perspective for the future. If you stay focused on your thoughts, you will find out that they were often just taken over. They might not always be your own phrases, mostly they`re adopted from others, who brought you up or were involved in the process.

If, on the other hand, you believe:

"People are bad,

I always meet the same weak character."

...this will hit you like a boomerang in the feedback, that you can only see in the world what most closely corresponds to your own assessment of things, people and situations.

Every pot has its lid, but here also in a negative way. Engrams, imprinted sentences that act as memory paths that guide the life of every person, are neutral in themselves, they are completely based on us. We can reformulate our sentences with the simplest of means, life is based on what we whisper to it - in self-talk. Let's not allow communication to break off, let's keep talking to life, which has no resentment towards us. We make an impression and life carries it out. Just as a friendly word to others shapes our relationship with one another, a friendly word to ourselves is the *game changer* for everything we want to see in life.

Life knows no limits for our goals, dreams and plans. When you consider how much people can achieve, financially, profession-ally, privately, there is abundance in all areas. Why should you be disadvantaged? The phrases of others, that bring them pros-perity, abundance and personal happiness can also be your phrases if you start by formulating them according to your ideas.

What phrases do you say to yourself when you have achieved your goals? These are the exact phrases that you need to internalize now to reach your goals, because everything that exists is always happening now. And that is the definition of reality, the magic of which you just need to recognize. If crises can arise from incorrect communication, is it possible to resolve crises through correct communication? The answer is: yes, of course. Sometimes one word is enough for the argument to start, escalate and drive people apart. You can't get over what someone said, and you must get even with the person, institution or whoever it concerns. If words have such power, why not use them in the right place so that they work and resolve crises? If you are confronted with a situation of solidarity and put yourself in the other person's shoes, how can you still hate?

What I say shall be done...!

...has little to do with magic, but more to do with the desire to shape and design your own life. To do this, you must first have the courage to deceive yourself, to convince yourself of something that is not yet there, not visible. Believing in the invisible, holding on to it is exactly the method with which you have learned everything in life so far, even if no results were visible at first. We learned to walk, talk, ride a bike, swim, read and write, math, and later a profession. Many of us have learned to raise children and have not taken a course or received any educational training to always do everything right. We often grow into things because we must or because they are expected. And fortunately, things often work out exactly as we wanted them to - because we *wanted* them to!

When a child stands on its feet for the first time and then staggers unsteadily around the room, you would assume that there is an incredible will and a lot of courage behind it to undertake this venture. But the child approaches the matter completely carefree and does not give up, even if it keeps falling - one day it will stand and then be very proud of itself. The inner phrase could be:

"I want to walk, and I know I`m going to get there!"

And the words become actions, at least first attempts, as is the case with all of us when we learn something new, but the older we get, the more discouraged we seem to be. We no longer must conquer the world, or we are tired of it, considering all the experiences we have during a lifetime. And then maybe at some point you just want to rest. Like an old cat by the stove. And then that is exactly the goal. But if you still want to change things in your life and haven't put your hands in your lap yet, then the right sentences can help, even if you know that they are bringing the future into the present.

Realizing something you have planned, simply because you can repeat the right phrases that relate to the present on a regular basis, is your own contribution to fulfillment that you have already made in advance.

Why shouldn't you wipe away the past and re-educate yourself, but this time according to your own ideas?

A Strategy for Millions of People

A large part of humanity lives according to memory structures that are unwanted, unloved and harmful. The chance to lay your own future by laying a new foundation in the present holds the potential for this large number of people to shape their lives with reference to their own ideas or at least lead them in new directions. We are made up of phrases and follow them every day. Just as the route to work or to the supermarket is controlled by the subconscious mind, we behave almost blindly in all other areas of life according to established programs, based on sometimes very old routines. We have stopped questioning our phrases and instead live with unsatisfactory situations, privately or professionally, and do not know how to change them.

The principle is:
This phrase, this direction,
another phrase, another direction.

The new phrase should dominate the day, become a part of you in repeated form, just as the transformation then becomes a new part of you. If millions of people take this to heart, and countless people are already doing so by no longer being willing to hold on to their old habits, then this world will be a better place for all of us. Because the happier people there are, the fewer we will be confronted with wars, hunger, crime and problems. The more people no longer feel controlled by others, but rather self-determined, the better people's relationships will be in their friendships, partnerships, at work and in the family. If you want to erase old tracks and leave new, better tracks, you must have a new education that you want and that you create yourself. There is nothing wrong with changing your own educational program if it means you will have a better, healthier and richer life. Who would say no to that?

But the shadows of the past have left their mark and sometimes we have developed unhealthy behaviors that harm us. We numb ourselves with food, alcohol, smoking or other coping strategies. If we change the program, meaning the phrases in our head, we can also change unpleasant, ingrained routines that have become addictive for many people - for example cigarettes and sugar. In the following practical section, I describe how you can tackle these problems with new memory pathways. The decision for new strategies must be made and after that phrase, which mirror this new outer pathway on the inside, can be formed and repeated constantly. How long? Until they become a part of you, that you do not have to mention any longer but just do the job automatically to your advantage.

Abracadabra in practice

smoke-free & slim

Calm down

Becoming a Non-Smoker by the Right Words

I have smoked cigarettes since I was a young teenage girl, and in difficult times I even smoked thirty cigarettes a day. I have often tried to quit smoking, but it only lasted for a short while, then I was back to it. For me it seemed impossible to quit.

When I think that I have not smoked for seven years now, I can hardly believe it myself. The puzzle that so many people must deal with, namely, how to stop smoking, can be reduced to a small common denominator: It is once again the *one phrase* that is crucial, that determines whether you turn your money into a blue haze and waste it senselessly, or whether you prefer to fly to the most beautiful beaches in the world, go on holiday and enjoy life and breathing freely.

But stop!

The most beautiful beaches in the world are already taken, because the managers of the tobacco industry relax there and laugh secretly, although of course they would never do that openly. They smile and joke about the smokers who ultimately make all their wealth and fancy holiday destinations possible for them, because smokers all have the same problem. They believe very often a day, to be precise, for four to five minutes each time, that the cigarette they have just lit could somehow help them to cope with their lives. I can say that because I know what I'm talking about, and I know that the problem goes deeper.

Unfortunately, the supposed lifeline is nothing more than an illusion. The only thing the cigarette offers is a portion of neurotoxin, administered through nicotine, which over time weakens self-confidence and mental capacity, so that you must smoke more and more in order to be able to tolerate stress at all. You don't get stronger, on the contrary, you become more and more thin-skinned.

Nicotine causes you to lose the ability given to you by nature to set boundaries, to use your defenses and to stay cool when things get heated. In the USA there is a saying: "Anyone who smokes is weak!" This refers to the mental state, the lack of self-discipline and self-esteem of those affected.

Smoking Takes Away Your Self-Confidence

But people are not weak in themselves, smoking is what made them weak in the first place. Nicotine causes the loss of inner strength, along with all its other harmful substances.

As an example: I once had a colleague who had to constantly go outside his office to smoke. If she had made a phone call that lasted just five minutes, she felt forced to go straight back outside to light the next cigarette. She had lost so much of her independence that she could hardly survive without her self-chosen "straw". Every little challenge had already weakened her as she was used to not solving stress out of her own inner sources but always clinging to the cigarettes as if these were people in the background, who borrowed her their strength in certain moments.

**The reality is that cigarettes are not helpers,
indeed, they are killers.**

The more you hold on to something, the more you lose your own strength. If you then rely on yourself again (i.e. when you stop smoking), your self-confidence grows in parallel, like a plant that has been standing in a dark, airless room for too long and is now allowed to see the sunlight again.

When I tried to quit smoking every few years, I was always amazed that after I had stuck with it for some days, I not only breathed more easily, but also became much more self-confident. Then, when I got a little stressed, the house of cards collapsed again, and I resorted to the old addictive substance.

Smoking steals your money

I remember an acquaintance of mine at the time who bought a pack of cigarettes every day for 10 Euros (that is 3.600 Euros a year). When everyone else around him took their well-earned vacation in the summer, he usually stayed at home. His standard saying was:

"I can't afford a vacation. I don't know why.
I must be doing something wrong."

And so, he went around in circles and there was no hope of improving the situation.

At another time, much earlier in his life, probably when he was young, he had learned phrases like:

"When things get difficult in life, just light a cigarette, it calms you down so you can stay cool!"

Unfortunately, being sick, poor and dependent is not cool at all. The following sentence would have been better for him:

"It's better to be healthy, fit and independent, then you'll be strong enough in difficult times!"

Or you behaved in stressful situations like the famous cartoon man who always reached for a cigarette when he was angry. The advertising slogan from that time, which was played as a matter of course on radio and television, was:

"Hold on, my friend! Who's about to blow up? It's better to reach for the... (Name of cigarette brand)!"

Consumers who believed the media's *educational mission* followed this and completely forgot what it's like when you simply start solving your problems by yourself with some stress management methods instead of delegating them to a drug which then has its customers completely in its hands. I call smoking a drug because you cannot just stop. That is the nature of drugs - you cannot give it up easily, you are addicted, and you spend all your money, often your shirt off, on them because it gives you what you need the most – self-confidence.

Anyone who sees it differently should think about how often they have driven to the gas station late at night because the pack of cigarettes was empty. Normally, it would never have occurred to them to peel off their pajamas at that time, get dressed and head out around midnight - all in the service of addiction. Remembering that you can get by on your own in life, that you are stronger than you know right now, that you can deal with stress without any aids

- this knowledge alone is the first step to being able to stop smoking.

But we believe the usual sayings that smoking calms you down, is cool, promotes community and lets you "be part of it". These learned mantras have a life of their own and so it happens that smokers often say they cannot imagine life without cigarettes. But they do not really need the nicotine so much as to them there is no other statement they could believe in instead.

It is so easy to change your attitude and look at things from a different perspective. This doesn't mean telling yourself that you don't like smoking anymore. I didn't stop because I didn't like it anymore. But I realized a certain fact and that was the turning point. For years the cigarette industry sold me a product that quickly became addictive and made me sick in the years that followed. And should I pay for that too?

The Truth is: You have been screwed!

I was no longer willing to fall for them, after all I had already paid a fortune to the industry and suffered various health problems that I did not usually associate with smoking but that were related to it, nonetheless. I realized that I had fallen for a very clever, subtle and at the same time terrible illusion that was sold to me in the form of cigarettes, leaving me addicted, paying and sickly for the rest of my life.

I successfully resisted this, I no longer wanted to be taken for a fool!

One day I realized that the managers of the cigarette industry were taking my money and my health from me and they didn't care at all about how I felt. That they were making money off me every day, selling me a product to which a substance had been added that was quickly addictive and that I was now condemned to give these people an amount x every day for the rest of my life (10 Euros or more?) - forever and ever!

I realized that they had tricked me, that they had sold me nothing more than a homemade lie - the illusion that smoking could make something or anything better. But it's not true - there's nothing good about it, it only has disadvantages.

In 1993, the book *"Allen Carr's Easy way to Stop Smoking"* was a global bestseller. In it, he correctly described that smoking does not taste good and does not smell good either, as many smokers often claim. The positive feeling comes from the fact that a drop in the nicotine level in the blood means that the substance that you need to get the level back to the level you need to stop responding with withdrawal has an illusory positive effect on the sensory organs such as the sense of smell and taste. But smoking is simply repulsive in terms of taste and smell. Only the smoker does not notice this because the addiction permanently clouds the truth and senses. Anything that helps to eliminate with-drawal symptoms is quickly perceived as good and right. The body reacts with positiveness because it feels freed from the burden of the feeling of lack but claiming that smoking tastes good shows how much you have already been manipulated.

I had tried many methods to stop smoking myself, but nothing helped. It was only with my own "therapy" that I managed it, and it still seems like a miracle to me today, but it was very clearly outlined, planned and calculated. Because everything else didn't work for me, all the well-meaning suggestions, methods and practices didn't work, I needed something else to be able to leave my soul comforter. I had to create self-manipulations that enabled me to stay with my strengths in critical situations and not to resort to any aid. I had to learn to recognize difficult moments as such, to anticipate my typical reactions and develop tactics to be able to deal with them.

When you become aware of what smoking actually does to your body, how much money you waste through it, how many years you could potentially die earlier, how often you were ill and didn't associate it with smoking and yet you were infected, caught a cold, sick and broken, precisely because smoking destroys the immune system and the body can no longer protect itself adequately. The daily practice and glorification of this disease-causing addiction has no justification and must finally stop. It is time to change your mind about it.

The most important questions I asked myself in this context were: What can I do when stress comes? What can I do instead of smoking, how can I react to it differently?

The tips that came to mind were:

• Drink a glass of water
• Jog around the block once
• Go to the open window and take a deep breath
• Hit a punching bag
• Hit a pillow
• Go into the woods and scream
• Do some exercise
• Do more exercise
• Buy a bouquet of flowers
• Buy new clothes (more reward)
• Meditate
• Do yoga, and so on.

But because none of that worked for me, I thought about what happens in the body when I'm stressed, angry, disappointed, sad, resigned, raging, etc., and how the feelings that are so unpleasant disappear again. I needed a strategy! I also had to integrate new thought patterns, phrases and engrams. So I designed a two-step rule:

Step 1:

At the beginning of every change there is a change in attitude, a phrase that describes what you say when you have achieved your goal. For me it was the phrase:

"I will no longer allow myself to be exploited, made ill and taken for a fool by the cigarette industry!"

To be honest, I really don't like it when someone tries to trick me, take me for a fool or lead me by the nose. And that is exactly what happens to smokers every day that they do not turn away from their imposed addiction, which is very lucrative for the industry. If you think that the cigarette industry manager is a cool guy who rides a horse through the desert and seems to be damn aloof and above all, then that may be true. But in reality he is damn clever, because he himself is a non-smoker. And while the smokers continue to believe in the false promises of stress reduction, he is of course lying on the beach in the sun (at the smoker's expense) and enjoying himself. He or she simply orders the next cocktail and laughs about how millions of people (smokers) have fallen for his or her scam. If you continue to smoke, you are also financing these people, their luxury holidays, sports cars, real estate, etc. But you keep losing money and even become ill with no ending in sight.

Step 2:

There are two components of addiction:

1. Physical addiction and

2. Mental addiction

To stop smoking permanently, you need the following "tools": In addition to the daily phrase that expresses the feeling/thought when you have achieved your goal, you also need something that relaxes the mind and something that relaxes the body. Because if you want your smoking cessation to be more than just temporary, you need a good strategy, because we are dealing with a strong opponent here. A true friend does not take money out of your pocket and accepts that you will get ill. You should say good-bye to such *friends*, you do not need them. You would never stay in contact with such people in real life, unless you are masochistic or - addicted.

Against Physical Nicotine Addiction:

Every year in autumn I had a bad cold, which left me completely out of action for almost two weeks. My doctor always told me that it was related to smoking. If I didn't smoke, my immune system would be stronger, I would get only a little cough now and then, a little runny nose, but that was all. I didn't believe her at the time. For smokers, such comments feel as if others don't want to be-grudge you your favorite activity and are making fun of it - as if they want to take something away from you!

In fact, it is like this: I have been smoke-free since July 2018, which is about seven years as of today, and I must say quite clearly that I have not had a cold since then. A little cough, a little runny nose during the cold season, that's all.

The doctor was right.

Nicotine Patches work

In terms of physical nicotine addiction, *Nicotine Patches* supported me in this time of abstinence. However, you really must use them for three months and not stop after one or two months because you think you're over the hill. There's a reason why it's set for this period. If you stop using them too soon, the withdrawal symptoms may return with full strength, and you'll end up resorting to the old "aid" to feel normal again. That's why, in my personal experience, it's better to stick to the medically recommended period.

I had almost no withdrawal symptoms from day 1 of using them and that of course made it easier to stop smoking. You should remove them overnight, otherwise you could overdose - after all, smokers don't smoke at night either. It's best to get detailed advice from a doctor or pharmacist before you start using them. Not having to constantly deal with annoying physical deficiencies is of course very helpful on the way to becoming a non-smoker, because you have enough to do with the mental component, which also requires a certain amount of strength. Being free or almost free of physical withdrawal symptoms helps to make the entire process of quitting easier.

Against mental dependence:

You should be aware that feelings are nothing more than *chemical reactions* and that such chemical explosions in the body work for a while, make a person suffer, happy, sad, crazy or overwhelmed, but then eventually fade away again. I have never seen anyone who was angry forever, until the end of their life, forever annoyed or stressed and never calmed down again. The truth is so simple, but we always look for the most difficult solutions to our problems, because what seems difficult is probably also difficult to deal with, we believe. If stress and all the other negative feelings, as described, subside over time, then you don't really have to do anything to avoid them. After all, they go away on their own, so why drink a glass of water, go for a walk, try yoga, meditate, count to 10, drink tea and so on and so forth? It should then be enough if you just do the following - namely:

NOTHING!

Whenever I couldn't deal with unpleasant feelings and resorted to one measure or another (i.e. smoking cigarettes as a coping strategy), I resolved that next time I would not chew gum or drink coffee or buy flowers instead of smoking - I simply did …

NOTHING.

Simply staying calm, noticing the feelings and being sure that they would soon disappear again, I made it my new habit. The excitement, the tension, the feeling of being overwhelmed, the nervousness can only be traced back to a hormone release that is responsible for the unpleasant feelings, yes, triggered them. The hormones migrate into the blood and, so to speak, "get it going".

Get Your Nervous System Back Down – Without Any Substance!

This is the moment when you believe you must take action so that the blood can flow more calmly, and you feel better. Whenever you resort to a substance in certain situations or just out of boredom, be it alcohol, pills, other drugs, cigarettes or anything else that has a calming effect, you are showing a reaction to the specific situation, whatever it may be. Then the drug, the substance, the cigarette or other things would have lost their power over you. But as soon as you react, the substance wins. It's like a struggle for power. Who is in charge? The drug or you?

If you don't react in times of stress, i.e. don't consume anything in response to it, don't smoke, don't drink, just do nothing, stay calm and wait until the inner storm passes, and by the way, it always does, if you manage to do that, you have already done the main part of the way to becoming a non-smoker, non-drinker, etc. You show practically no movement and say to yourself:

"Calm down – relax!"

You refrain from any activity, distract yourself mentally or wait until the hormonal surge caused by anger, arguments, disappointment, rage, sadness, stress subsides again. And it will subside.

The smoker doesn't know that. He or she thinks that they must smoke so that the unpleasant feeling subsides. But it does so anyway. Smokers must learn not to react, to let the problem (when everything has been resolved on a factual level) pass. Smokers must learn to deal with unpleasant but also pleasant feelings differently. In truth, you don't have to use anything to calm yourself down. It's also enough to do nothing, not always react immediately, not move, when you understand that a bad mood will turn into a good mood again after a while.
It´s a matter of time, try it out.

Don't habitually turn to addictive substances because you think you won't be able to cope with the storms of life otherwise. The truth is - you can do it. Even without taking action - and smoking again.

Many alternatives in behaviors or habits can be helpful, but what is the point if a new addiction develops from this? Then you jump from out of the frying pan into the fire. The goal is to become mentally free and not to exchange one problem for another.

"Unpleasant feelings disappear over time anyway –
you don't have to avoid them by smoking cigarettes!"

Anyone who has never learned to deal with feelings, whether positive or negative, is more likely to always look for something to hold on to, to avoid the feelings and deal with them as best as possible. The body reduces the negative feeling over time, it goes away, definitely - even if you do nothing about it, try to stay calm, just do nothing and feel the emotion-causing hormones breaking down from the blood.

So, my strategy was to do nothing when anger or stress arose. Just try out what happens if you don't immediately fall back into activities like eating, drinking, smoking, swearing, complaining, crying, screaming. All of that can have liberating effects for a moment, but unpleasant feelings are ultimately just feelings, they go away again after they have raged inside you. At some point, feelings get tired too.

That can be good or bad. For the smoker who must learn new strategies for dealing with stress, it is a blessing when he finally has some peace. The old memory paths are imprinted deep in the layers of the brain and from there act like an autopilot and let people almost stereotypically carry out the same actions repeatedly if the worst comes to the worst. It's the same with new paths - the more often you follow them, the faster they become automatic actions that no longer feel strange. Everything is basically a learning process, smoking and not smoking.

"Just stay calm, do nothing.
Calmness returns, it always does, sooner or later."

The brain prefers to stick to its routine of smoking rather than quit because of health risks. Sometimes a spark of logic comes into one's consciousness, and you realize how bad smoking is. But then the habit takes hold again and you function like a

programmed robot. Smokers have stopped questioning their behavior, they don´t doubt it anymore. And why should they? All they
get from outside are clever lectures instead of helpful and concrete suggestions for using new strategies that work better and
at the same time do not harm health or wallet. The alternative
stress management method against psychological dependence
is simply to stay calm, wait and not become active or to not slip
back into old behavior.

"Wait and see! And (not even) drink tea."

You might get addicted to the idea, that you can cope feelings
with tea – and still believe that it would be necessary to consume
something. So then next time it might be the cigarette again what
you think you need to compensate stress or other factors. If you
take nothing the brain gradually understands more about how
strong and independent it really is and that it never needed a cigarette to cope with the negative situations in life. Even if you didn't
learn beforehand how to best deal with stress, sadness, anger
and annoyance. But you can learn it afterwards - you are never
too old to achieve new things, and it is never too late. To be honest, I have a lot less stress today because I am much stronger
mentally than when I was a smoker. I get upset less, don't let

things get so close to me and have had to learn to get over feelings like frustration, grief and anger without any help.

Recognize your emotional smoking

When I was a child, my family and I lived in a small social housing apartment with three rooms on 68 square meters - father, mother, my three older sisters and me. We had no window in our small bathroom and my father liked to smoke a cigarette while he shaved in front of the mirror in the morning. When I went into the bathroom afterwards, I could still smell the cigarette and see the ash in the sink. Becoming a smoker myself had connected me in a deep way with my father, who I could be close to in an indirect way, because the smell reminded me of him and of the now-empty bathroom with the ash in the sink. The smell in the morning had become something positive for me and so it was only a matter of time before I started smoking too. My parents had separated and of course I missed my father. But he was always there for me when I needed him. He probably also felt guilty towards me that he couldn't be there and that I had to grow up without him. However, the more often he helped me with something, the more dependent I felt over time. His support, which was well-intentioned, made me more and more dependent. Sometimes we miss a person and we turn to something else instead, a substitute, in moments when we feel overwhelmed and need that person the most. Being able to stop smoking also means being free, no longer needing a "straw" and being able to rely on the most important person in your life from now on, a person who will always be there for you 100% - rely on yourself!

The best way to quit is to choose the right phrases and repeat them every day. Smokers have engrams that keep them addicted. Non-smokers have other engrams that describe and reflect their life without addiction. The phrases that you say to yourself every day are those that guide and lead you - they give you the direction and you act accordingly without thinking about it any further, because they have long since become your classic habits that you no longer rethink or question. *"If it has always been like this, then it must be the right thing"*, you believe.

Habits can be changed when you get to the root of them, i.e. change the words that once led to this exact habit and now have a life of their own.

The Anti-Smoking Phrases

There are classic memory pathways that hold smokers captive and automatically make them continue to pursue their addiction. These unconscious beliefs come from a time when it was normal to resort to certain means to be able to cope with everyday life, which was perceived as overwhelming, often seen when people suffered from trauma of any kind. They apparently did not know that they were fundamentally strong enough in the first place.

The beliefs that can lead to addiction are as follows:

- *"I can't do it alone, I need a tool for everything, I'm just too weak."*
- *"The only fun I have is smoking cigarettes all the time."*
- *"Smoking is getting more and more expensive, but I'll find the money somehow."*
- *"I'm sick, I'm coughing quite often, I can't get up the stairs, but I'll just keep smoking, so what."*
- *"After all, you have to have some kind of vice."*
- *"Alcoholics are worse off, but nobody complains about that, only about smokers, that´s not fair!"*

New memory paths for non-smokers,

with which you can stay addiction-free and have a better life:

- *"I'm glad that I'm keeping my health and my money."*
- *"I'm so happy that I'm now part of the non-smoker group."*
- *"I'm very relieved that I've managed to become a non-smoker."*
- *"From now on, I am strong enough to no longer allow myself to be exploited by an industry that makes me poor and sick."*
- *"Thankfully, I do not take any substances that harm me or lead to addiction."*
- *"I really enjoy living a healthy life and make sure that I maintain this status."*
- *"I will never again support companies that take money out of people's pockets and promote their illnesses."*
- *"My money belongs to me, and it will stay that way!"*
- *"Why don't I smoke? Because I'm not stupid!"*

You shouldn't formulate the phrases as something that will happen at some point or soon. Don't say: *"I should stop"*, but:

**"I AM a non-smoker, and I AM just so happy
about how good it feels."**

If such learning content is repeated daily, over a period of several weeks, i.e. until it has become a matter of course, then the body reacts with a natural affirmation. The phrases that the smoker had once learned were ultimately also initially internalized to convince him or her that smoking was so great that he would spend a certain amount of money on it every day, invest a certain amount of one´s life by doing it, and allow cigarettes to simply destroy large parts of their health. All because of a few words that were learned through repetition and that now define this important part of life.

In the end, all it takes is a series of better words to reverse the process.

Personally, I have never felt the need to smoke again since I had stopped. Sometimes I am asked whether I don't think about the time when I was smoking and wish I could have a cigarette again. To be honest, I never have these thoughts or feelings. Not at a party, not when being with others and certainly not when I'm stressed or angry. I'm far too happy that my self-developed therapy worked. How could I ruin it again? Definitely not. And I have completely forgotten what it was like to be a smoker and what it felt like - I never expected that myself. But it is possible - with a good plan, a well-thought-out strategy and the right words.

Abracadabra

What I say, shall happen!

"I am now a happy non-smoker!"

Magically Slim Yourself

Lose Weight with the Right Words

You Are Already Slim!

It is in your nature to be slim.

There is almost nothing better than waking up in the morning feeling fit, looking in the mirror and realizing how toned and beautiful your body is. You have the desired clothing size, your jeans fit, your T-shirt sits well. Your waist is defined, your legs are in good shape. If you need a certain item of clothing for an important event soon, you will simply buy it. It is that easy. And that is how it should be. Nothing else exists. Faith moves mountains. For you, only this way of living should be counting. You were slim in the beginning, that is your pure nature. It is exactly the state that brings a smile to your face when you think about how well your body weight and height match.

Your Thoughts Determine Your Weight

Harmony is your constant state. When you think about what to cook today, you will choose a delicious, easily digestible dish that is rich in vitamins, low in fiber and low in fat anyway. This is your life, your thoughts, your joy. Every other way of thinking about your previous eating habits gradually dissolves until one day it disappears completely. More and more every day. Some people drink Coke in the morning, but certainly not you. Some start the day with fast food, you don't. Some people must eat something sweet every now and then, but you don't. Some people eat and feel guilty about it, unlike you. You treat yourself responsibly. You don't need any of these. You see yourself as slim and that is why this will be your normal state if you don't let yourself be dissuaded from this vision.

If you are on your way to work in the morning and suddenly you get caught in a traffic jam on the motorway, only one thought will count for you: *"I mustn't be late. No, absolutely not! That mustn't happen. What will others think of me then. Oh God, I hope* this *damn traffic jam clears soon!!!"*. You say to yourself: *"I'm late!"* and your behavior follows this thought, because what you focus on is exactly what life serves you on a silver platter. In this life you can only ever get what you see, feel and consider important. You will be late that day because your thinking no longer allows any other option. There could have been the thought: *"I can do it. The traffic jam will clear soon. Absolutely. I'm sure I'll be on time today."* And that's what would have happened.

Many overweight people swear that diets don't help. They believe that the cravings will keep coming back anyway, or they try to numb themselves by eating when they're in a bad mood. Then it was all for nothing again, all the drudgery in the gym, the abstinence, the constant weighing, the controlled eating. But because thoughts determine weight, the attitude manifests itself very quickly and the diet has no result. We are not looking for the perfect diet, we want the right thoughts because they are the only solution to excess weight, just as the wrong thoughts were the actual cause of excess weight, and this created an unhealthy cycle – which then determined and controlled your eating behavior.

When you leave the house, several images and impressions rain down on you. Fortunately, we have a filter in our heads that sorts these impressions into important and unimportant. We would not be able to process all the colors, things, people and would be completely overwhelmed if it weren't for this supervisor who tells us what we need and what we don't. The "sorter" in the brain filters the impressions according to relevance and experience. So, when you are stuck in a traffic jam, experience tells you that being late can have unpleasant consequences and that it is important to be on time. That is why your inner supervisor immediately sets off all the alarm bells that cause you to change your mood and behavior. You panic and perhaps try to push on the highway. This in turn can lead to dangerous situations that could only have arisen because you filtered the single idea of *"I'm late!"* Then this single phrase works like an autosuggestion that will sooner or later become a fact in your life. Our thinking determines how we live, how we behave and what we get back from life in the end.

The slim person thinks slim. Food nourishes him or her and of course he or she can also enjoy it. But since food is not necessarily the topic that thoughts constantly revolve around, the body can also release a lot of the calories it has consumed; they have no greater significance for it. So, what exactly is important to you? How do you filter? What do you pay the most attention to? What you perceive belongs to you. If there are several categories to choose from on the website, such as astrology, chat corner, blog, diet club, friendship club, partner search, competition, fashion and others, then if you are not happy with your weight, you will probably first direct your attention to the category *diet club*. Perhaps this happens unconsciously and is a clear sign of how you see yourself. Namely as someone who has a connection to the topic of diet. And of course, your body will follow this special perception. It cannot do otherwise, because the brain controls the body's functions and only ever carries out what you believe in.

Your Body from Back Then Is Still There

That's why the topic of diet club should no longer be a topic that you pay attention to from now on, because after all, you are moving your perception more and more day by day towards the person you have always been and who has perhaps been taking a nap inside you far too long. Instead, concentrate on everything you want to achieve. Direct your perception towards the future, rather than the past and the things in your present that bother and burden you the most. It is your slim self, your light, happy being, that will not show itself if you believe that it is not there. Because you can only ever see what you believe in. Everything you do not believe in will not show itself to you either. Therefore, believe that you can awaken your slim self from its *Sleeping Beauty* sleep, that you can remove the thorns that it encloses through the simple means of a new perception.

Your body from back then is still there, the hips, the waist, the chin, the neck, the knees, the hands, the stomach, everything is there, but it is difficult to recognize as such. It is the self-made shell that encloses your body and had a good purpose on the one hand. But the more you understand that you don't need this shell, the more you dare to face life, the less you need the protection you have built up, which is supposed to act as a kind of armor to protect people from external threats.

Because you usually don't start eating too much in good times, but rather in the times when you need attention and healing. The shell should protect you from all the unpleasant experiences that we can all be exposed to daily. But this is also an illusion. Again, we fool ourselves into thinking that we can evade the responsibility of having to face our problems. We withdraw, make ourselves "comfortable" and in doing so only reinforce the basic conflict.

We reward ourselves for the hard week, give ourselves all the good, beautifully packaged and sweet things, even if we then must pay a price for it in the form of excess weight and health problems. If we change our inner sentences, then we will manage to behave differently, making different decisions. Because the background is again our false beliefs.

If you want to lose weight now, you must transform yourself into a person who

- thinks of the right phrases and repeats them until they become second nature
- is not afraid of the problems this world presents
- no longer needs a protective shell
- no longer lets negativity take the lead
- is willing to give positivity more importance in life
- directs selective perception towards everything that benefits the body and soul rather than harms it
- wants to start showing the self in the original form again, and that was and is – slim!
- feels confident enough to face life courageously
- plans more exercise units into everyday´s life in small steps
- believes in what is coming, more than in what is currently stressful
- does not give up and continues to hold on to the new phrases
- recognizes success due to the changed inner attitude and is thus further strengthened to hold on to the new

Slim Phrases:

"I only let good and pleasant impressions flow through my mental filter."

"I only see what I want to see, especially my slim self."

"It is in my nature to be slim. That is how I was intended, that is how I was created. Being slim is my natural state."

"I free myself of all the ballast that I have acquired over the years."

"I no longer need an external protective armor. My good thoughts protect me."

"I see myself in a new, improved form."
"I no longer think about the burden of the past."

"My health and well-being are more important to me than the effort that is demanded of me."

"I protect myself from stress every day as best I can."

"At the same time, I avoid unnecessary burdens."

"This new day has a wealth of wonderful moments in store for me."

"Even in the morning, I put myself in a positive mood for everything that shapes my everyday life today."

"Every good thought burns off excess body weight."

"From day to day, my thoughts are increasingly directed towards the side of the world that has so much beauty."

"I know that this world also has dark sides, but I choose to be part of the sunny side through thoughts and behavior."

"Through people like me, this world becomes a little more beautiful every day."

"I greet the lightness of the new day in the morning and say goodbye to the heaviness."

The encouraging words of the famous French pharmacist Émile Coué (1857-1926) have proven their worth and helped customers who picked up their medication from him and were given a special phrase to take with them:

"You are getting healthier and healthier every day, it will be always better and better."

For all other facts, plans, and sensitivities, you can also use this phrase structure with the right wording:

"I'm getting slimmer every day."

"I'm getting healthier every day!"

"I'm feeling lighter every day!"

You can effectively incorporate the idea of self-suggestion into your everyday life and observe how it has a positive effect on your inner self and over time creates an image that brings inside and outside into harmony.

We construct an ego that is freed from harmful influences and can feel new and slimmer.

Positive Thinking as An Alternative Diet Aid

How you speak to yourself is how life, the environment, and people speak in an indirect response that creates situations, reactions and events. The better you treat yourself, praise yourself, take care of yourself, expect positive things, the more of them you will see on the outside, the more of them you will embody yourself.

Too much of the wrong fat is harmful to the body. This can lead to heart attacks, depression and circulatory diseases. Certain facts are not healthy. The more you consume them, the more unbalanced your mood becomes, and the same goes for sugar. A fat-free self can become a fat-laden self - and vice versa. A person who tends to be in a good mood can then become a grumpy person - but conversely a bad-tempered, pessimistic person can become a happy, optimistic person.

It is not so important to always analyze the previous problems that led to obesity. You can burn fat in the truest sense of the word if you simply focus your thoughts on the good things in life. We are always faced with a choice. If you spend a few minutes in the morning getting in the mood for the great possibilities of the new day, you strengthen your immune system and arm yourself against verbal attacks from outside and other negative influences. Good thinking to start the day means choosing a salad with chicken instead of a ham and chips, it makes people choose refreshing table water instead of sweet lemonade. Good thinking makes the difference. Good thinking helps you lose weight. It is so easy to see beauty in everything, just do it.

"The dose makes poison."

Paracelsus
(Alchemist; 1493 - 1541)

The body needs around 60 - 70 grams of fat per day. It is equally important to let off steam during the day, when necessary, to allow yourself to be angry, annoyed and negative. If you constantly think positively about everything and everyone, you become out of touch with the real world. There are bad things in everyday life, it is important to let the positive prevail without getting caught up in illusions that distort reality.

What fat is to the body, frustration is to the soul. You get to work and try to reduce body fat, so that you can relieve the burden on your soul and become happier. But it is much easier to work directly on your soul. Seeing things positively has the same effect on your psyche as a vitamin boost does on your body. The more you look at everyday things positively, the more you do good for your body, because it always follows your mental state.

A Good Thought Is Like an Apple You Eat

A day full of good thoughts is like a load of vitamins and more healthy food for your body. Good thinking has the same effect on your body as a weight-loss diet. The more you manage to free yourself from negativity, the more you lose weight on a physical level. Positive thinking requires less discipline than a diet. Positive thinking immediately shows its effect in a good mood. Diets take time and are often difficult to stick to because you don't see the results straight away, you feel bad about it and become easily discouraged.

The more positively you look at things, the more the body will, in the analogy, only take from food what it needs and what is good for it. New thinking does the same. It only filters out from the environment what is usable, useful and not very stressful. Body and mind are always one. You should bring them to a new common level. But as long as you pay more attention to the things that are wrong in this world, and there are a lot of them, the body will continue to focus on the substances that are actually harmful to it when it takes in food, it will obey and demand what fits with the negative way of thinking of people, i.e. all the things that are unhealthy and give the illusion of temporary happiness. This explains why some people can eat whatever they want without gaining a lot of weight. Others get fat from even the smallest bite. Of course it is also a question of metabolism, but who controls it? You yourself, your brain - ultimately your subconscious.

The soul plays a significant, if not the most important, role in the state of the body, whether in terms of health or its shape and size. You can use this knowledge by starting to feed your soul all the spiritual fruits, vitamins and other good products and substances, paying particular attention to the good and beautiful things in your environment: and this is much easier than any diet.

Fat makes the soul sick. You just thought that you could feel better if you treated yourself to something nice in a difficult life situation, e.g. a cozy dinner with fatty meat, creamy sauce, carbohydrate-rich side dishes and a sweet dessert, a cake in the afternoon or some candy and cookies in between. But it is precisely the very fatty foods that put a heavy burden on the soul as well as onto the body. Apart from the fat that the body needs, any excess is a means of increasing frustration and making people mentally ill. And so, they must eat even more because they still believe in the illusion that *what is tasty is good.*

The alcoholic drinks more and more because he or she believes that what calms down once will also help the next time, the time after that, and the time after that. However, the high consumption of a substance causes the body to suffer more and more over time, and beyond that the soul does not find what it is looking for - and that is peace.

Good fat in certain quantities is important for maintaining bodily functions. The overfat self, however, suffers from the physical and mental burden, the lethargy and the sadness caused by fat. The burdened heart seeks release - and yet again looks in the wrong place: in eating and consuming even more fat. But rethinking and changing this "bad habit" is not that difficult. Instead of counting calories, checking the fat content of food when you buy it and trying to hold back when you eat, there is a much more comfortable way: Get rid of excess fat on a physical level by first getting rid of excess negativity on a mental level. Nourish your soul with positivity, your body will follow suit and adapt to the new situation

- hasn't it always done that? A little fat is important, and so is a little negativity. We can't always swallow everything; we must bang on the table sometimes and assert ourselves. That is liberating and we make our position clear in our professional and private life.

"Everything that is a burden will be eliminated from now on. The good things can stay and will increase. You should be slim and healthy."

We don't want to convince ourselves with a new, positive way of thinking, we don't want to give in to the false belief that the world is nothing but beautiful and wonderful. That would be fatal. But - we can decide to focus more on the good than the bad. In this way, we bring better things into our lives. We cleanse our soul of all the superfluous things that burden us and, unconsciously, give our body a new command to be slim. Our body does not lead a life of its own. It obeys us constantly. Let us use this knowledge and make things easier for ourselves. If we concentrate our thoughts more on the beautiful things in life, we will brighten up, reduce our frustration, eliminate the very fat that our body does not need and become the way life intended us to be – slim.

This Is How the Psyche Influences Metabolism

All you must do is change your mood, your thoughts and ultimately - your perception. It's a child's play. Of course, there is the death of whales, there is war, environmental pollution and much more that can put you in a bad mood just thinking about it. But there is also sunrise, a fresh breeze in the morning, a call from a nice person, a hot coffee when you wake up, a few pretty flowers in the meadow, a tree in full bloom, a new day waiting to be conquered by you. Thinking about it can put you in a good mood. How do you decide what you want to perceive and how do you keep falling into the trap of negative thinking that gives you even more of what makes you rounder instead of slimmer?

This raises the question: Do you have to completely block out the bad in this world? Not entirely. Because it is good and sensible to devote yourself to charitable causes, to help people through donations or concrete measures that are within your own means. However, it makes less sense to constantly and continuously deal with all the suffering in this world. In the long run, this does not bring about a solution. It is therefore better and healthier for the individual to constantly reinforce the good. The less negatively you think, the more excess weight you have built up over the years through negative thinking will fall away. Every good thought burns fat. Every negative thought creates disharmony in the head and stomach, puts a strain on the soul as well as the body and manifests itself as excess fat, which is harmful and makes you unhappy.

- Why do some people gain weight even though they eat too little rather than too much?

- Why do others lose weight even though they eat more than enough?

The answer is not in the right or wrong diet, it is in the choice between happy and unhappy thoughts. Simply constantly force yourself to pay particular attention to the good in life, in your life, to the goal of being slim, to the beautiful clothes you will then wear, to the better body feeling, the increased mobility, the good immune system, the ability to exercise without effort, the healthy cardiovascular system and, last but not least, the fact that you feel more attractive. All of this is yours if you hold on to it and simply throw away any thought that conjures up images that contradict your own. Being overweight is the expression and result of unhappy thinking. Being underweight has the same causes. The ideal weight is achieved when height and weight are in harmony with each other. Every inharmonious thought will have an impact on your body weight over time, just as every inharmonious thought will put more and more strain on your soul over time. A lot of inharmonious thoughts can make you depressed and, as a physical reflection of this, can also make you fat. So, the underweight person is in the same predicament as the overweight person – in both cases there is no harmony.

Some people eat too much when they are sad, other people eat too little in the same situation. Perception is focused on experience and importance. So, if you want to lose weight, your consciousness tells you that it is immensely important to you, but your experience keeps getting in the way because you have probably already tried a lot of things to achieve your goal. But it is precisely this experience that leads to the inability to maintain the belief that the goal will be achieved in the long term. The negative thoughts keep trying to come back to you and lay in your path like paving stones. It is about consistently allowing a new way of thinking, planting the new image of the degreased self in your life once and for all, regardless of the perception of yourself you were previously used to. Your selective perception determines the world in which you live, it creates it according to the images you produce in your head.

You decide entirely on your own which images and thoughts you create, invite and allow. You can always decide for yourself what you want to think about and how you view yourself and your world. The positive attitude in the morning for the new day makes you less susceptible to all the events that may come your way. What's more, it is precisely this positive attitude that makes you strong and practically directs the filter in your brain to all the good things that will give you even more positive thoughts and an improved self-image. These thoughts need to be held on to, all others are superfluous and harmful, they drag you down energetically. And over time your body will adapt to the new, positive way of thinking, it has no other choice as you have already implanted a new routine on how you look at the world you live in.

Faith Puts Pounds Away

Strengthening phrases and positive formulations create a new reality. They make us believe in the good and adjust our inner being to it. When we are sick and in pain, we strongly believe that this pain will last forever. We believe that it will always be like it is, when we are in a bad state. But – pain will pass, wounds will heal, discomfort will disappear if we and our subconscious minds prepare for it in advance. Sometimes we want to give ourselves a little consolation. This can be a present that we give to ourselves, an extra day off that we can spend in peace. Something nice, something that should fill the gap of loss. Our perception, which is shaped by our experience, tells us immediately what can help in a hurry: a piece of chocolate, a warm lunch, a cream cake in the afternoon, any reward for the pain. Sometimes we go overboard.

And yet we know that the pain will go away even without the treatment. We don't have to resort to old and unhealthy behaviors to soothe the current pain. The pain is controlled by the head; if we relax it, we don't need to do anything for the body. It calms itself down when it receives command from the brain. So, it's not about soothing the unpleasant physical feeling in stressful situations, but rather about acting in the area that triggered the unpleasant physical feeling in the first place: our perception! We can return to our actual state with the right phrase and with a healing message.

"I want my figure back
from the time when I was younger!"

- is a phrase that leads to having more inner strength in critical situations to be able to resist sweets etc.

One day I was sitting in the waiting room of a doctor's office. It was full and all the chairs were occupied by waiting patients. Then the door opened, and a woman was supporting an elderly, frail man who was obviously very ill. Immediately, several younger patients got up from their seats to give the older man a chance to sit down. With a groan and a moan, he sat himself on one of the chairs and calmed down. The woman who had accompanied him stopped, looked around and then suddenly said something magical:

"Now things can only get better."

And then there was no longer the feeling that there was someone who had to be dealing with an illness, the aura of the old man changed into quite the opposite. *"Now things can only get better!"* caused the pitying looks of the other patients to change into looks full of hope and confidence. A general nod went through the room, along with a smile that said:

"If you see it that way, then that's how it will be."

And I too suddenly had the certain feeling that the man would soon feel better again. With this attitude of confidence, mountains can be moved, goals achieved and pounds burned. Then what is it that makes us go to the gym, improve our eating habits, go for a walk and want us to get the weight of the old times back? It is always a plan that we no longer want to stay in this condition, that makes us feel bad, look bad and runs us even more down. Losing weight is no big deal for your body. It is extremely adaptable and always does what you tell it to. Since the body is flexible in this respect, from now on we should only give it good orders rather than bad ones. Here are some examples:

Bad mental orders:

Human: "*The method doesn't work anyway. I'm not losing weight, I've tried everything.*"

Body: "*Make the method ineffective. Will be carried out without further ado! The order is: don't lose weight. Okay!*"

Human: "*I've always had a few extra pounds on my ribs, that's completely normal and shouldn't really be a problem.*"

Body: "*A few extra pounds, no problem. Sure. I'll do it!*"

Human: "*It's all so delicious, but I'll gain weight back straight away anyway.*"

Body: *"No problem. Get back on weight straight away. Will be carried out!"*

Human: *"The clothes I wore back then don't fit me anymore."*

Body: *"Clothes aren't supposed to fit. OK, if you say so, then it is true!"*

Human: *"I don't find these thin people attractive at all."*

Body: *"Well, keep your own pounds. Thin is not attractive. OK, boss."*

Human: *"If I eat this piece of chocolate now, I'll gain weight."*

Body: *"No problem. Turn the piece of chocolate into fat and attach it to my hips. I'll do it."*

Every thought of failure flows as a command from the head into the body and shows its results here. New, better thoughts do the same. Your body doesn't care what you think either. It always carries out your commands, it trusts you to give it the right instructions. If you want your arm to rise, it doesn't think about whether it's right or wrong, the brain just does it. You give the command; your body never questions what you do, it adapts consistently to you. Every command is preceded by a thought. Every conscious and unconscious belief affirmation has an effect on the body, which is why it is so easy to believe the right thing and then experience the result in the truest sense of the word "firsthand".

Good mental commands:

Human: "*I want to fit into this dress.*"
Body: "*It's easy, boss! Come on, your bodily functions, lose weight!*"

Human: "*I don't see why I should stop wearing a bikini at the pool. I can still afford it!*"
Body: "*Maintain or restore bikini figure. Yes, done!*"

Human: "*I can eat something sweet now and then, no problem.*"
Body: "*Eat something sweet - no problem. OK, I'd be happy to do that!*"

Human: "*I'm getting slimmer every day!*"
Body: "*Very happy to perform this! You`re getting slimmer every day. At your service.*"

The reason why your figure is not yet what you want it to be is because in the past you gave your body bad orders rather than good orders. No diet can help if your thoughts tell you otherwise. Magically slimming yourself means that you send the right orders directly to your body with good thoughts, because it only ever does what you tell it to, whether consciously or unconsciously. If faith can move mountains, tear down walls and heal illnesses, then it can also easily lead you to where you want to be most: in your new, slim self.

Times when we are plagued by existential worries are often unavoidable. We then believe that we don't have enough of anything. We are not (emotionally) satisfied. So many things need to be done, paid for, sorted out so that we can continue to live carefree. Sometimes there is not enough money to keep our own material situation balanced. Then we start living in our worries. Some of them may be justified and require a healthy rethink and the creation of new plans so that we can get our financial situation under control. Other worries are overloaded with thoughts of *"what if..."* and are therefore unnecessary.

When we are afraid of hunger and hardship, we tend to protect ourselves, we start to hoard. With the last of our money, we stuff the fridge full of unnecessary food so that we have enough of everything. We eat disproportionately a lot more than we usually do and especially consume the substances that are harmful to us and give us a feeling of unpleasant fullness. We build a safety barrier around ourselves, a protective wall, a lifeline. We want to save ourselves from shortages that probably won't even occur. We wake up at night out of sheer worry and pounce on the fridge. Just like babies who want to be sure that their mother is still available with her vital food, that she has not gone and abandoned her child. But we are in abundance, provided we live in countries that can feed their populations sufficiently.

When the situation improves, we quickly realize how unnecessary panic and worries were. But now we have a lifeline that we can't get rid of so easily. In addition, there is usually a feeling of guilt because we have once again resorted to our old and unhealthy measures. We start the next diet, do without, avoid, crave food - and then just eat more. Is there a life without worries? Probably not. But there are ways to deal with worries in a different way.

In fact, we get everything we need to make our living today. Just as we will get everything we need tomorrow, and the day after tomorrow, and next week, and the week after that too. We don't have to take hasty steps to avoid worries. Everything is available in abundance. Or could one say that there is a food shortage, at least here in the western world? Hardly. And there will be enough for us too. Only when you believe, there is a shortage, it will soon come up to you because, what you say, shall happen.

If we have existential problems, we will find a way to solve them today, tomorrow or the day after tomorrow, maybe next week or next month. We will have negotiations with people or institutions that can help us to eliminate the problems and put our worries aside. We can then place the problems in the hands of a higher power, trusting that everything will turn out for the best. Hasn't that always been the case?

From the time the worries arise to their solution, we go through a phase of uncertainty. These phases of life are often unavoidable. But they have an end, they pass. An important fact is how we have treated ourselves in the meantime. We don't have to do more than the current day is telling us to do. For today, it's enough and we will have plenty of everything. It will be the same tomorrow. With our worries, we focus on what we fear losing. Like a self-fulfilling prophecy, we increase the likelihood that exactly these cases will occur. Our selective perception always leads us to the places and situations in life in which our strong feelings do come true. There are also better places and situations, but we only ever see what concerns us most. We block everything else. This is not our own fault; it is how we were brought up. We live and think as we were told to do, even if it`s bad for us – as our environment didn`t know better we shouldn`t blame people who had no other ideas but theses ones.

If we believe that we must hold on to food, food becomes the center of our lives. If we believe we have the strength to hold on to ourselves, our own person, in all its strength and beauty, it becomes the new focus of our lives, replacing the old, harmful way of thinking. It can be damn comfortable to hide from the world, to extend the life preserver and to work even harder to strengthen the protective cushion.

But it is much more worthwhile to participate in life, to be active and to get out of the comfortable cycle of drawing the curtains, turning on the TV, putting your feet up, letting the sun wash over you, to get out and live your life. We cannot become slim if we hide from ourselves. We can do without the life preserver of our soul and at the same time the life preserver around our waist will fade away if we start to help shape our existence: by making this world more beautiful through our new, positive influence, at least our own, very personal world and the way we see it. Between 2003 and 2006, the *Robert Koch Foundation* carried out a study on the prevalence of obesity in our society on behalf of the German government. The results showed that obesity was more prevalent among socially disadvantaged people and those with a migrant background. The risk groups included children and young people whose parents were also overweight, so it could be assumed that this is hereditary. However, children whose non-biological parents are overweight are just as affected by obesity; an outcome that has been linked to previous experiences of an incorrect lifestyle and diet.

Happiness is out of reach. Unemployment, financial problems and social disadvantages dominate everyday life. The food industry promises a "sweeter" life in its colorful advertising if you buy and consume its products. A sad lie that backfires. The truth is different: increased consumption of fat does not make life better; it makes it worse. However, the dilemma cannot be solved by the convulsive compulsion to do unloved exercise and painful abstinence from certain foods. Anything compulsive causes an understandable, inner defensive attitude in people. To lose weight, people need a new vision of their future, which, in addition to expanded opportunities and perspectives for an improved life, naturally includes a healthy diet and lifestyle. Nobody said that there is no hurt, disappointment and sadness in this world and this life. These events happen if we allow them to - and then again there are events that are simply not our fault. We always have the choice of whether to put ourselves in situations that bring up and reaffirm old feelings or whether to change our self-image and thus redesign our lives.

Perhaps you remember phrases from the past that were intended to portray you as weak and inadequate. It is particularly painful when these sentences and statements come from the closest and most important people - that is extremely hurtful. *"You are too stupid for that, you can't do anything, you can't manage anything, let it go."* Then we want to ease our pain, and just as we continue to live with the hurt today, we repeat the attempts to ease it from back then. The mother cooked a nice lunch that gave us warmth and security. That felt good. A part of us then thinks that the disbelief in our own strength, in our own "rightness", is closely linked to the "rightness" of the food. Hurtful sentences and statements often come from people who themselves have little self-esteem. They have high expectations of others, of us, of you. If everything doesn't always work out the way they would like, we must take responsibility for it, we must pay for their mistakes.

But now a new time has dawned. The old injuries must be over. And only when we integrate this new time into our lives, when we make the big promise to ourselves not to allow unnecessary injuries anymore, will this constant cycle come to an end.

"I have been hurt, I am sad. Now I can eat, I deserve it."

...is a sentence that must become a thing of the past.

"I will not allow others to hurt me. I fundamentally reject that. Not with me. That stops now."

...is a phrase that initiates new thinking, one that can prevent new, inappropriate injuries in the future.

You don't need a diet to get out of this self-harming cycle. You need to reject further injuries, increase self-respect, the desire to see yourself internally and externally in a new way to eliminate all the false and superfluous phrases and statements from others who do not respect themselves at all and that is why they must blame anybody for their problems – in this case it is unfortunately you. And then it is no longer so much about losing body fat, it is about losing an old, superfluous opinion that aims to transfer low self-esteem to us by hurting us so that the person who expressed it can exonerate themselves. We are not dumping ground for the weaknesses of others. Let us forgive these people and stop allowing new hurts.

Let us say *NO* to a life that burdens us with the weight of hurt.

Let us say *YES* to a life that relieves us of the phrases and statements of others by no longer allowing them to hurt us.

Phrases of Self-Respect:

"Every day I learn better and better how to protect myself from the hurt of others."

"I fundamentally reject phrases and statements from long ago, as well as new ones, that shame and humiliate me. Get rid of them!"

"Food is not my way of resisting the urge to feel warm inside. My new, high level of self-respect gives me a much greater warmth."

"Eating as a reaction to hurt is wrong and does nothing good for me. My new self-respect as a reaction to pain heals me in a healthy way."

"Every day I am becoming more and more of a person who respects him/herself."

"I respect myself and treat myself well. I have these high expectations of others too."

"I set clear boundaries for those who use me as a dumping ground for their weaknesses."

"It's getting easier to respect myself every day."

"As my new self-respect increases, the excess weight is getting less and less, every day. I don't need it anymore."

"My figure from back then is still there, I want to see it again, I want it back!"

"Every day I feel more comfortable in my own skin, my weight is leveling out again."

Space for your own phrases:

_____

_____

_____

_____

_____

_____

Fear of Calories Can Get You Overweighted

Whenever you count calories, you make them important and thereby bring them into your life even more. *Selective perception* can be focused on everything. If you focus on everything about your person that is not so perfect, you give the deficit power - they become bigger and stronger. Everything that you don't find so great about yourself, your personality, your appearance, you can make smaller by taking away this power, this attention. Focus your attention on everything about you that is beautiful, that you like. And in doing so, you give power to the good in and about you. Now this is becoming more.

Selective perception leads to what is known as "tunnel vision". People can then only see the things in their environment that confirm their assumption that either most things are good, or most things are bad. Focus this tunnel vision on the good and the good that is there anyway will mostly come into your focus. If you focus your vision on the negative, which is also present in this world, your natural perception will only filter out the negative from everything that exists - to your own detriment.

Here is an example: Simon drives a car with summer tires in all weathers. Somehow, he never has the money to finally buy and fit the tires he needs for winter. So, he drives with summer tires on black ice, snow, and mud and doesn't think about it anymore. When the law on the use of winter tires is tightened, Simon finally must convert his car. But he takes his time because he doesn't have the money for the tires yet. Now he continues to drive around with inadequate tires, feeling guilty and afraid of a police check. Then one day his *selective perception* changes. The journey seems excessively long to him, he is restless and worried, feels bad and guilty. He pays particular attention to the tires of many cars that drive past him. He asks himself: "*Can you tell with the naked eye when someone is still driving with summer tires? Can you tell whether the tire has the right or insufficient tread depth just by looking? Which streets and which areas are freer of snow than others? Is there a better, safer way to work, to go to the supermarket, to see a friend?"*

Simon's attention makes him forget everything else around him; he only looks at other people's cars and tires and is ultimately happy when he gets home. The winter drive with summer tires was dangerous, but it was made even more dangerous by Simon's tunnel vision, which made him a strained and anxious driver who, in this state, almost "focused on" the dangerous situations. When Simon finally gets the winter tires he needed fitted a few days later, he drives calmly and relaxed and no longer sees the other drivers' cars and tires but concentrates on the traffic and driving safety as he usually does.

Something similar happens when he eats. If you think you are overweight and feel guilty and bad about it, you will send a message with every bite:

"You are a burden to me!"

Your body will understand that eating is something that makes you heavy and harmful, and so it will transform the bite wrapped in a negative message into an actual burden that is not good for the body. Therefore, focus your perception on the fact that food is powerful and important to sustain life. Choose high-quality and nutritious food that enriches you and makes you feel good. With this decision, your body will tell you every time its needs are met and when you have had enough.

Focus your perception on everything that is already good and beautiful about you and your life - and make exactly that stronger and bigger! Looking in the mirror will show you many things about your body that are good, right and beautiful. If you consistently pay attention to these areas, your *selective attention* will give your body the command to become even more beautiful.

It is not difficult to focus on your beautiful hands, shoulders, knees, posture, fingernails and everything else about you that is already the way you want it to be, what you want and what you can love about yourself. *Selective perception* automatically increases everything that you pay the most attention to.

- If you concentrate on the negative aspects of your body, you make them stronger

- If you concentrate on the positive aspects of yourself and your appearance, you strengthen them

See your beautiful sides today and increase them in the process. Turning away from what does not correspond to your ideal image and you make it smaller and smaller until it dissolves on its own. If you pay attention to the calories, you give them weight. If you pay attention to the beauty in you instead, it will find its way to you to a greater extent. We see what we want to see. We perceive what we want to perceive. Of all the millions of impressions we are exposed to every day, our brain only filters what it thinks is important and appropriate. We do not see the factory worker who toils away on the night shift if we have no personal connection to it. We do not see the cleaners who clean the supermarket at six in the morning if we have no connection to it. We do not see the homeless person sleeping under the bridge if we have no connection to it, or we see it shortly and as we don`t have this connection we have forgotten the picture in a few seconds.

We create our own world from everything we have or want to have a relationship with. Our brain filters - and that is a good thing, otherwise we would be overwhelmed if we had to see, recognize, perceive and process everything that exists around us. If we are not happy with our appearance, our brain starts to filter here too. We see what is not ideal, we see ourselves as over-weight, we focus on the extra pounds on our hips and flabby upper arms - at the same time we ignore what is right about us. The brain filters and reinforces what it considers to be particularly important. Since we are all perfectionists in a way and have a need for happiness, beauty and well-being, we particularly look at the things about ourselves that do not meet these requirements. We see ourselves as fat. But that is not a final judgement that we have to make about ourselves. We can give our brain a new task. Ultimately, we decide for ourselves what and how much our brain should filter.

Fear can be good, right and lifesaving. It is a natural impulse that protects us. But - if we are afraid of gaining weight, it becomes a vicious circle. We want to lose weight but still must keep eating. Then we feel guilty, get confused and eat even more out of fear and insecurity. The more we focus on this cycle, the more weight we gain. It's about weakening the increase, reducing the fear and focusing the perception of being fat on being slim.

Fear is caused by holding on to the old and not allowing the new. Fear is caused by staying overweight because it has become a habit to perceive ourselves the same way and not differently. We must change this perception. We must change our way of thinking. Let's practice only seeing what we want to see and then observe what results from that. Let's practice recognizing the beauty in ourselves, what is good about us, instead of focusing on the imperfections. The more our perception focuses on the positive aspects of our appearance, the more we reinforce this beauty that every person has. Then we reduce, diminish and eliminate fat, the padding, the unnecessary weight, which does not serve any purpose, is superfluous and makes no sense. We don't need it. It should go away. Bye. Get rid of it.

Anyone who consistently focuses on the beauty of themselves will automatically want, attract and get more of it. On the other hand, anyone who consistently focuses on their excess weight will automatically get more of it, attract more of it and become a victim of their own perception, plagued by fears and the resulting self-harming compulsive behavior.

We exchange fear for trust. Trust in our own perception, the certainty that if we direct our focus in a new direction, we will get more of what we want, become more of who we want to be and basically already are.

Why does one person live in a different world to their neighbor? Why is one slimmer and another fuller? Is it always just genes, wrong eating habits, upbringing, external temptation? If we believe that overeating is something beautiful and positive and provides mental comfort, then we are victims of our own *selective perception.*

We believe what we want to believe - and act accordingly. This excess of food ultimately has the opposite effect to what we want to achieve. We feel burdened, overburdened and restricted. It is possible to train your own perception and renew it by changing your view of things. When you are craving a chocolate bar it's because you have directed your perception to the term "chocolate bar". Then a simple calorie bomb in crackling paper becomes the most important thing on earth.

It is like when a woman who desperately wants a baby only sees pregnant women everywhere. The lonely person sees happy couples everywhere, provided he or she wants a new relationship. Once you've had enough of it after a breakup, you no longer notice the couples. After all, you don't "want" to see them.

A man who is unhappy with his physical shape suddenly sees bodybuilders everywhere. If you have a new boyfriend/girlfriend with a purple car, you will get the impression when walking through the city that there are loads of purple cars. But that's not true, it's just your own perception that always shows you most of the things, people and events that you really "want" to see. Because of this "filtering" perception, you only ever notice on the outside what you have the strongest inner connection to.

And so, everyone lives in the world that they most support, even if unconsciously. Therefore, a changed appearance can only ever come about through a previous change in inner perception. New decisions must be made, which then produce their results on the outside. Just as the old decisions once resulted in excessive and unhealthy body size, a change in perception together with renewed behavior can make the desired goals a reality.

When should you start making a new decision? When is the right moment? How can you force yourself to think in a new and different way? It is good to set a fixed date, starting next Monday, starting next week, and not to fear this date, because - from then on you don't have to do without anything, but from then on you get something new and better.

Words for the Soul

*"I see the beauty in me.
I want it to increase."*

*"My perception is focused on the fact
that I am getting slimmer day by day."*

*"I give my body the sufficient nourishment
it needs to function, nothing more."*

*"I give my soul sufficient nourishment by concentrating
on the beautiful and wonderful things about
myself and my appearance."*

"I am getting slimmer day by day anyway!"

*"I am sure that I will reach my goal. Nothing stops me.
Everything is good."*

"My focus is on my slim self."

*"My tunnel vision is consistently focused on the fact that
so much about me is good and beautiful."*

*"Day by day, I am increasing the beauty
of my appearance."*

"I have confidence in my own perception – and my perception constantly shows me all the beauty that makes me who I am."

"Of course, I enrich my life with regular exercise, which strengthens and beautifies my new self and keeps me at a fit level."

"I am replacing old, damaging feelings with new confidence in myself and my body."

"My perception is now exclusively focused on achieving a new self-image that is healthy, fit and slim."

"Of course, I am managing to refocus on the beautiful and great things about me."

"I am replacing fear with trust and am actually becoming more and more positive day by day."

"I am so happy, I started the new sports program, which takes the stress away and cheers me up every time I exercise."

"I feel so much better now that I lost weight."

In Conclusion

Choose your phrases carefully –
they might come true ...!

Positivity is good energy. It converts fat into muscle mass. Positivity gives you strength. The best strength training is useless if your soul is weak. This irritation makes the body sick, the heart cannot be deceived. Treating yourself well does not exclude treating other people well. That is why friendliness is an important factor. Greeting the new day, greeting the people around you, what does a smile cost? Every form of good thinking and acting brings you closer to your dream shape, inside and outside.

Walk whenever possible, avoid the elevator, take the bike instead of driving, consistently choose the option that is more positive for your body and soul in everything you do. Focus your attention on everything that is good, unburdened and without the excess fat that the body doesn't need. Your perception is your life, and you perceive what you decide to do every day.

What you believe, what you say, what you think and what guides you has been reflected in your life ever since you were shaped

259

by your parents. Everything you are today, what you own and what you represent in life and in society is an expression of the phrases you have learned, which have a life of their own because you have stored them through repetition. This process happens either intentionally or automatically. Today you can decide for yourself which influences should be predominant for you, and life will reflect this accordingly.

It makes sense to weaken bad impressions, to let them be as best as possible so that they are "pushed to the sidelines" and to strengthen and consolidate certain new impressions so that over time an existence becomes more and more what it should have been from the beginning - your beautiful, rich and worth living life.

The more people remember this, the more beautiful this world becomes. And I very much hope so, always think about it, repeat this thought so that it becomes ingrained and what I say soon comes to pass:

Abracadabra - this world is good.

Literary and graphic sources

Beattie, M. (2003). *The Language of Letting Go: A Meditation Book and Journal for Daily Reflections*. Hazelden.

Dihle, A. (1987). *Die Schicksalslehren der Philosophie in der Alten Kirche.* In: J. Wiesner (Hg.): *Aristoteles. Werk und Wirkung.* 2. P. 52–71

Eicher, H. (2017). *Die verblüffende Macht der Sprache: Was Sie mit Worten auslösen oder verhindern und was Ihr Sprachverhalten verrät.* Springer.

Festinger, L. (1954). A Theory of Social Comparison Processes. In: *Human Relations*, Nr. 7, P. 117–140.

Fuchs, T. (2013). "The Phenomenology of Affectivity", in *The Oxford Handbook of Philosophy and Psychiatry*, Oxford: Oxford UP, 612–631.

Fuchs, T. (2018). Zwischenleibliche Resonanz und Interaffektivität. *PDP Psychodynamische Psychotherapie: Forum der tiefenpsychologisch fundierten Psychotherapie, 17*(4), 211–221.

Frakes, J. C. (1988). *The Fate of Fortune in the Early Middle Ages: The Boethian Tradition*. BRILL.

Fuchs, T. (2009). *Das Gehirn - ein Beziehungsorgan: eine phänomenologisch-ökologische Konzeption*. W. Kohlhammer Verlag.

Gluck, M. A., Mercado, E. & Myers, C. E. (2010). *Lernen und Gedächtnis: Vom Gehirn zum Verhalten*. Spektrum Akademischer Verlag.

Goddard, N. (1944). *Feeling Is the Secret*. Goddard Publ. USA.

Kohnstamm, O. (1915). Demonstration einer Katatonie-artigen Erscheinung beim Gesunden (Katatonusversuch). In: *Neurol. Zentral Bl.* 34S, 1915, P. 290–291.

Krockow, von, C. G. (1958). *Die Entscheidung: eine Untersuchung über Ernst Jünger, Carl Schmitt, Martin Heidegger*. Stuttgart

Landmann, M. (1971). Eine Lanze für das Schicksal. In: Ders.: *Das Ende des Individuums*. Stuttgart. P. 208–214

Lenzen, W. (1994). *Realität und „Wirklichkeit"*. Kritische Bemerkungen zu Gerhard Roths „neurobiologischem Konstruktivismus".https://www.philosophie.uni-osnabrueck.de/fileadmin/Allgemeine_Uploads/Publikationen/Lenzen/Realitaet_und_Wirklichkeit.pdf. Retrieved on 09/22/2024

Luhmann, N. (1984). *Soziale Systeme: Grundriss einer allgemeinen Theorie*. Suhrkamp.

Maier, S. F. & Seligman, M. E. P (2016). Learned helplessness at fifty: Insights from neuroscience. Psychological Review,123 (4), 349-367.

Marquard, O. (1977). Ende des Schicksals? In: Ders.: *Abschied vom Prinzipiellen.* Stuttgart 1981. M. E. Reesor: Necessity and Fate in Stoic Philosophy. In: J. M. Rist (Hg.): The Stoics. Berkeley

Meltzoff, A. N., Moore M. K. (1977). Imitation of Facial and Manual Gestures by Human Neonates. *Science.***198**,75-78. DOI:10.1126/science.198.4312.75

Neubauer, S. & Burkhardt, K. M. (2024). *Glück ist Hormonsache: Der natürliche Weg, um Körper und Seele in Balance zu bringen und psychischen Leiden gezielt entgegenzuwirken.* Riva.

Roth, G. (1994). *Das Gehirn und seine Wirklichkeit.* Suhrkamp.

Schmucker, M. & Köster, R. (2014). *Praxishandbuch IRRT: Imagery Rescripting & Reprocessing Therapy bei Traumafolgestörungen, Angst, Depression und Trauer.* Klett-Cotta.

Schulthess, R. (1959). *Ich, Freiheit, Schicksal.* Tübingen.

Stangl, W. (2024, 25. Juni). *Engramme als Basis des Gedächtnisses.* https://psychologie-news.stangl.eu/4711/engramme-als-basis-des-gedaechtnisses

Van der Kolk, B. A. (2014). *The Body Keeps the Score: Brain, Mind, and Body in the Healing of Trauma.* Viking

Watzlawick, P. (1976) *Wie wirklich ist die Wirklichkeit? Wahn, Täuschung, Verstehen.* Piper.

Information about the author, book and seminars:

www.ingridtrier.de

In social media:

 https://www.instagram.com/ingridtrier_/

 @ingrid_trier

https://www.facebook.com/ingrid.trier.520/